Preaching the Miracles
Cycle B

By John R. Brokhoff

C.S.S. Publishing Company, Inc.
Lima, Ohio

PREACHING THE MIRACLES, B

Copyright © 1990 by
The C.S.S. Publishing Company, Inc.
Lima, Ohio

Library of Congress Cataloging-in-Publication Data

Brokhoff, John R.
    Preaching the miracles. Cycle B / John Brokhoff.
        p.   cm.
    ISBN 1-55673-251-1
    1. Jesus Christ--Miracles.   2. Bible. N.T Gospels--Homiletical
use.   3. Jesus Christ--Miracles--Study and teaching.   4. Common
lectionary.   I. Title.
BT366.B74   1990
251--dc20   90-35200
                                                                              CIP

9039 / ISBN 1-55673-251-1   PRINTED IN U.S.A.

Contents

Tables

Introduction

This book does not provide prepared sermons for anyone to repeat word for word. This would not be fair to anyone who wants to grow as a preacher.

Rather, this book on miracles is intended for the busy pastor who, week after week, year after year, is expected to prepare a sermon within a single week. It is for the preacher who can not take time from other important ministerial tasks to spend many hours per week considering what various biblical scholars have to say about a particular miracle. The purpose of this book is to help the preacher prepare an interesting and helpful message for the congregation despite his or her practical limitations.

The author of this book would like to consider himself your partner in sermon preparation by doing for you the ground work of exegesis, suggesting preaching values and ideas derived from the text, and by offering illustrative material for the sermon. The book is to serve as a homiletic springboard or as an airstrip for the sermon to take off from.

Three basic questions will be faced as we consider each miracle:

1. Is the miracle for real? Are we preaching a myth, a legend, or an historical fact?

2. What is the miracle saying to us? What truth is revealed? A miracle has a mouth; it is an enacted parable.

3. How can we relate and apply the miracle to everyday living?

Before beginning the preparation of sermons on the miracles, the preacher should think through the following questions:

1. Must one accept Jesus' miracles to be a true Christian?

2. Do miracles break the laws of nature?

3. Did the miracles actually happen?

4. Do the miracles prove the deity of Jesus?

5. Did Jesus perform the miracles to gain a following?

6. Are Jesus' miracles different from other miracles?

7. Can one sincerely preach on a miracle without believing that it happened?

Miracles of Jesus
in the Common Lectionary

Miracles by Jesus

Sunday	Miracle	Matthew	Mark	Luke	John
Lent 4(A)	Man Born Blind	—	—	—	9:1-41
Lent 5(A)	Raising Lazarus	—	—	—	11:32-44
Pentecost 11(A)	Feeding 5,000	**14:13-21**	6:30-44	9:10-17	6:1-15
Pentecost 12(A)	Walking on Water	**14:22-33**	6:45-52	—	6:16-21
Pentecost 13(A)	Demon-Possessed Girl	**15:21-28**	7:24-30	—	—
Epiphany 4(B)	Unclean Spirit	—	**1:21-28**	4:31-37	—
Epiphany 5(B)	Healings	8:14-17	**1:29-34**	4:38-41	—
Epiphany 6(B)	Leper Healed	8:1-4	**1:40-45**	5:12-15	—
Epiphany 7(B)	Paralytic Healed	9:1-8	**2:1-12**	5:17-26	—
Pentecost 2(B)	Withered Hand	12:9-14	**2:23—3:6**	6:6-11	—
Pentecost 5(B)	Stilling the Storm	8:23-27	**4:35-41**	8:22-25	—
Pentecost 6(B)	Two Healings	9:18-26	**5:21-43**	8:40-56	—
Pentecost 10(B)	Feeding 5,000	14:13-21	6:30-44	9:10-17	**6:1-15**
Pentecost 16(B)	Deaf-Mute	—	**7:31-37**	—	—
Pentecost 23(B)	Blind Bartimaeus	20:29-34	**10:46-52**	18:35-43	—
All Saints Day/ Sunday(B)	Raising Lazarus	—	—	—	11:32-44
Epiphany 2(C)	Wedding at Cana	—	—	—	2:1-11
Epiphany 5(C)	Catch of Fish	—	—	5:1-11	—
Passion(C)	Malchus' Ear	—	—	22:50-51	—
Pentecost 2(C)	Centurion's Servant	8:5-13	—	7:1-10	—
Pentecost 3(C)	Widow's Son	—	—	7:11-17	—
Pentecost 21(C)	Ten Lepers	—	—	17:11-19	—

Miracles of Jesus
in the Common Lectionary

Jesus the Miracle

Sunday	Miracle	Matthew	Mark	Luke	John
Advent 4(A)					
Christmas(A,B,C)	The Nativity	1:18-25	—	2:1-20	—
Epiphany 1(A,B,C)	Baptism	1:9-11	3:13-17	3:21-22	—
Transfiguration (ABC)	Jesus is Transfigured	17:1-9	9:2-9	9:28-36	—
Easter(ABC)	Resurrection	28:1-10	16:1-8	24:1-11	20:1-18
Ascension(ABC)	Ascension	28:16-20	16:19-20	24:46-53	—
Pentecost(ABC)	Holy Spirit	Acts 2:1-21			

Notes:

1. The only miracle by Jesus given by all four Evangelists: Feeding 5,000.

2. Only one miracle by the Father given by all four Evangelists: Resurrection.

3. Three miracles reported by John only: Cana, Man Born Blind, Raising Lazarus.

4. Three miracles reported by Luke only: Catch of Fish, Widow's Son, Ten Lepers

5. Over a period of three years, using the Lectionary; only two of Jesus' miracles are repeated: Feeding 5,000 and The Raising of Lazarus. (Both will be treated in *Preaching the Miracles; Cycle A)*

Miracles According to Lectionary Cycles

Sunday	Miracle	Reference
Cycle A		
Advent 4	**Nativity**	Matthew 1:18-25
Lent 4	**Man Born Blind**	John 9:1-41
Lent 5	**Raising Lazarus**	John 11:1-45
Easter	**Resurrection**	Matthew 28:1-10
Ascension	**Ascension**	Luke 24:46-53
Pentecost	**Spirit's Coming**	Acts 2:1-21
Pentecost 11	**Feeding 5,000**	Matthew 14:13-21
Pentecost 12	**Walking on Water**	Matthew 14:22-23
Pentecost 13	**Demon-Possessed Girl**	Matthew 15:21-28
Cycle B		
Epiphany 4	**Unclean Spirit**	Mark 1:21-28
Epiphany 5	**Healings**	Mark 1:29-39
Epiphany 6	**Leper Healed**	Mark 1:40-45
Epiphany 7	**Paralytic Healed**	Mark 2:1-12
Pentecost 2	**Withered Hand**	Mark 2:23—3:6
Pentecost 5	**Stilling the Storm**	Mark 4:35-41
Pentecost 6	**Two Healings**	Mark 5:21-43
Pentecost 10	**Feeding 5,000**	John 6:11-15
Pentecost 16	**Deaf-Mute**	Mark 7:31-37
Pentecost 23	**Blind Bartimaeus**	Mark 10:46-52
All Saints' Day/Sunday	**Raising Lazarus**	John 11:32-44
Cycle C		
Epiphany	**The Star**	Matthew 2:1-12
Baptism of Our Lord	**Voice from Heaven**	Luke 3:15-17, 21-22
Epiphany 2	**Wedding at Cana**	John 2:1-11
Epiphany 5	**Catch of Fish**	Luke 5:1-11
Passion	**Malchus' Ear**	Luke 22:50-51
Transfiguration	**Jesus is Transfigured**	Luke 9:28-36
Easter 3	**Post-Resurrection Catch**	John 21:1-14
Pentecost 2	**Centurion's Servant**	Luke 7:1-10
Pentecost 3	**Widow's Son**	Luke 7:11-17
Pentecost 21	**Ten Lepers**	Luke 17:11-19

Note: The major miracles (Festivals), consisting of the Nativity, Baptism, Transfiguration, Resurrection, Ascension, and Pentecost occur in each of the three lectionary cycles. If a major miracle does not appear in one volume of this series, it will be found in one of the other two volumes. For complete coverage of all miracles in the Lectionary, it will be necessary to have all three volumes of *Preaching the Miracles, Cycles A, B, and C.*

Types of Miracles in the Lectionary

Sunday	Miracle	Reference
Nature Miracles		
Pentecost 11	**Feeding 5,000**	Matthew 14:13-21
Pentecost 12(A)	**Walking on Water**	Matthew 14:22-33
Pentecost 5(B)	**Stilling the Storm**	Mark 4:35-41
Pentecost 10(B)	**Feeding 5,000**	John 6:1-15
Epiphany 2(C)	**Wedding at Cana**	John 2:1-11
Epiphany 5(C)	**Catch of Fish**	Luke 5:1-11
Easter 3(C)	**Post-Resurrection Catch**	John 21:1-14
Healings		
Lent 4(A)	**Man Born Blind**	John 9:1-41
Epiphany 5(B)	**Peter's Mother-in-Law**	Mark 1:29-39
Epiphany 6(B)	**Leper**	Mark 1:40-45
Epiphany 7(B)	**Paralytic**	Mark 2:1-12
Pentecost 2(B)	**Withered Hand**	Mark 2:23—3:6
Pentecost 6(B)	**Two Healings**	Mark 5:21-43
Pentecost 16(B)	**Deaf-Mute**	Mark 7:31-37
Pentecost 23(B)	**Blind Bartimaeus**	Mark 10:46-52
Passion(C)	**Malchus' Ear**	Luke 22:50-51
Pentecost 2(C)	**Centurion's Servant**	Luke 7:1-10
Pentecost 11(C)	**Ten Lepers**	Luke 17:11-19
Exorcisms		
Pentecost 13(A)	**Demon-Possessed Girl**	Matthew 15:21-28
Epiphany 4(B)	**Unclean Spirit**	Mark 1:21-28
Death to Life		
Lent 5(A)	**Raising Lazarus**	John 11:1-45
Easter(A,B,C,)	**Resurrection**	Matthew 28:1-10; Mark 16:1-8; Luke 24:1-11; John 20:1-8
Pentecost 3	**Widow's Son**	Luke 7:11-17
Pentecost 6(B)	**Two Healings**	Mark 5:21-43

Miracles of Jesus
Not in the Lectionary

Gadarene Demoniac	Matthew 8:28—9:1; Mark 5:1-20; Luke 8:26-39
Feeding 4,000	Matthew 15:32-39; Mark 8:1-10
Healing Epileptic	Matthew 17:14-20; Mark 9:14-29; Luke 9:37-43
Cursing of Fig Tree	Matthew 21:18-22; Mark 11:12-14
Two Blind Men	Matthew 9:27-31
The Dumb Demoniac	Matthew 9:32-34
Crippled Woman	Luke 13:10-17
Man with Dropsy	Luke 14:1-6
The Official's Son	John 4:46-54
Lame Man at Bethesda	John 5:1-18

Preaching the Miracles of Jesus

Despite our scientific and technological generation, we live in an age of miracles. They are so many, and they occur so often, that we tend to take miracles for granted. When one gets well from a serious illness, we say, "His recovery was a miracle!" When we see pictures of a car wreck, we say, "It was a miracle all were not killed." A wife sent a friendship card to her husband with the message, "You love me! Will miracles never cease?"

Every day we experience miracles. They are miracles because we cannot understand or explain them. For many a computer is a miracle of information. Can a cook explain the miracle of a microwave oven which heats the food without heating the oven? Is it not a miracle that on television a conference can be held with one participant in New York, another in London, and a third in Tokyo? With radio, television, radar, VCRs, and computers we live with miracles every day.

People are always looking for and expecting miracles to happen. On a recent visit to Lourdes, I saw approximately 5,000 people on litters and in wheelchairs hoping for a miracle of healing. In West Germany hundreds lined up to get water out of a well in Ranschbach when the news got out that the water had healed a boy's blindness and a seventy-year-old man's arthritis. In 1988, 3,000 people gathered at a Roman Catholic church in Lubbock, Texas to experience the miracle of the Virgin Mary's appearance with a message.

In *The Road Less Traveled*, Dr. M. Scott Peck reports his change of mind about miracles:

> *Fifteen years ago, when I graduated from medical school, I was certain there were no miracles. Today I am certain that miracles abound. This change in my consciousness has been the result of two factors working hand in hand. One factor is a whole variety of experiences I have had as a psychiatrist which initially seemed quite commonplace but which, when I thought about them more deeply, seemed to indicate that my work with patients toward their growth was being remarkably assisted in ways for which I had no logical explanation — that is, ways that were miraculous.*

11

In the light of this, should we be surprised that Jesus performed miracles? It is claimed that two-thirds of Jesus' active ministry was concerned with healing. In the New Testament there are thirty-five miracles by Jesus. In a three-year period, a preacher using the gospel lessons for preaching will be confronted with a miracle of Jesus on thirty-seven Sundays.

Before we attempt to preach the miracles, we need to think through the answer to a basic question, *Did the miracles actually happen?*

What is a Miracle?

Many definitions have been given for a miracle. The following represent a few of the most important:

St. Augustine: "A miracle is an occurrence which is contrary to what is known of nature."

C. S. Lewis: "I use the word, miracle, to mean an interference with nature by supernatural power."

William Barclay: "A miracle is an event in which God's power has made a special entry into our lives."

The Bible has no single word for miracle. Our word comes from the Latin, *miraculum,* meaning "wonder." The New Testament uses four Greek words for miracles:

Erga — works. The word refers to the mighty deeds of healing. (John 5:36)

Dunamis — power. Miracles result from the power of God in Jesus. (Matthew 11:21)

Semeia — signs. Miracles point beyond themselves to God's presence, the coming of the Kingdom, the new age and the downfall of Satan. It is John's favorite word for miracles. He used it seventeen times. (John 2:11)

Teras — wonders. The miracles caused people to wonder with amazement. The Disciples ask after the stilling of the storm, "What manner of man is this?" (John 4:48)

In Acts 2:22 Peter, in his Pentecost sermon, uses three of the words for miracles: "Jesus of Nazareth, a man attested to you by God with mighty works *(dunamis)* and wonders *(teras)* and signs *(semeia).*" Each of the four words for miracles refers to a characteristic of Jesus' miracles.

12

Objections to Miracles

1. Scientism. "I believe in nothing that cannot be explained to me," says the scientist. Since miracles cannot be explained empirically, science objects to miracles because they violate the laws of nature. They object to the idea that the supernatural invades the natural.

Thomas Merton described the closed system of modern science:

> *Science can do everything, science must be permitted to do everything it likes, science is infallible and impeccable, all that is done by science is right. No matter how criminal an act may be, if it is justified by science it is unassailable.*
>
> *(Conjectures of a Guilty Bystander,* p. 78)

In a closed system of naturalism, there is no room for miracles resulting from supernaturalism. Nevertheless, most Christians do not claim that miracles necessarily violate the laws of nature. According to Augustine, miracles may violate only what we understand of nature. Miracles may result from laws which we do not yet know about or understand.

2. Liberalism. Biblical and theological liberals often oppose miracles because they are supernatural. This position was stated by Rudolf Bultmann: "Today we can no longer regard miracle stories as evidence of divine intervention in the normal course of things. This puts an end to the New Testament miracles as miracles." For these people, the Gospels are not considered historical accounts. All supernatural references such as angels, demons and miracles need to be demythologized into existential terms.

How then do liberals explain the miracles? Though opponents of miracles have explained them as the results of demonic or magical sources, none has ever claimed that nothing happened. The usual response is to claim that the miracles were illusions. They try to explain away the miraculous element. In the case of the raising of Jairus' daughter (Mark 5:35-43), for instance, they claim that the girl was not really dead, only asleep or in a coma. For the miracle of feeding 5,000, one explanation is that the people shared their lunches with each other after witnessing the selfless sharing by the young boy. In the classic case of David and Goliath, a physician

13

explained that Goliath had a cyst on his forehead. This cyst was a soft spot which allowed the pebble to penetrate Goliath's brain, killing him instantly.

A Case for Accepting the Miracles of Jesus

In view of the objections of scientism and liberalism to miracles, can we still accept the miracles as actual historical events? Can we preach on them sincerely, believing in their literal validity? Consider the case for accepting miracles as historically true.

1. The integrity of Scripture. The miracles of Jesus are recorded in the Gospels. They are an essential part of the Bible which we accept as the written Word of God. The Bible is a reliable and trustworthy witness to the truth of God. This truth has never failed nor been found to be deceptive. The historical-critical study may show us how the miracles came from Jesus' deeds, through the oral tradition of the Apostles, and finally recorded by the Evangelists. But the reliability of the accounts is sure and acceptable. One can simply say, "I accept the miracles of Jesus because I accept the Bible as God's Word."

2. God's omnipotence. Miracles are possible because God is all-powerful. Jesus did not perform his miracles. God did them *through* him. In explaining how he cast out demons, he said, "If it is by the finger of God that I cast out demons . . ." (Luke 11:20) The infinite power of God the Father enables the Son to heal the sick, cast out demons, and walk on water. Yahweh asked Abraham, "Is there anything too hard for God?" (Genesis 18:14) When the Virgin Mary questioned how she, as an unmarried person could be a mother, the angel assured her, "For with God nothing will be impossible." (Luke 1:37) Often people healed by Jesus gave God the praise for the miracle rather than Jesus. (Luke 17:15; 18:43) If we believe in God Almighty, we can accept the miracles of Jesus.

3. The miracle man. Jesus is the miracle of miracles. His incarnation, resurrection and ascension are the greatest miracles. His being a miracle makes possible the miracles he performed. He is like the sun that makes possible our seeing the other planets, as they reflect the sun. Jesus' miracles are secondary and insignificant compared with the greatest miracle, Jesus Christ himself. We do not accept Christ because he performed miracles. Rather, we accept his miracles because he is Christ. If we can accept the "greatest miracle," there is no problem believing in his lesser miracles.

4. We cannot prove or disprove the miracles of Jesus. Ultimately, acceptance of his miracles depends on our faith. But it is not with blind faith, for we cannot believe in the reality of some so-called miracles. In the reported appearances of the Virgin Mary in Lubbock, Texas, August 1988, some women claimed that their silver rosary chains turned to gold. Likewise, who can accept the miracle concerning a medieval martyr who, after his head was cut off, supposedly walked to the cathedral with his head under his arm and entered the cathedral singing the *Te Deum*?

Miracles are accepted by faith, but it must be an intelligent faith, bishop David Jenkins explains:

> *Miracles are gifts, not guarantees, given to faith, and they always involve a mysterious collaboration and convergence between the intervening power of God and the human response of faith, obedience and activity.*

Reasons for the Miracles

Jesus was selective in performing miracles. He was not a miracle worker who made a miracle happen at anyone's beck and call. He did not perform miracles to display his power for the amusement of King Herod. When Jesus was sent by Pilate to Herod for trial, Herod was disappointed when Jesus refused to perform a miracle. (Luke 23:6-12)

Similarly, Jesus refused to enact a miracle when the religious leaders challenged him to prove that he was the Messiah. In response, Jesus said that no miracle would be given to an evil generation like his own except the sign (miracle) of Jonah. (Matthew 16:1-4)

There had to be a good reason for a miracle before Jesus would perform it. There was always a purpose for the miracle. What were some of the purposes?

1. To manifest the glory of God. The miracles of Jesus were not for self-glorification in terms of fame or notoriety. The miracle at Cana (John 2:1-11) and the raising of Lazarus were for the glory of God. (John 11:4) The miracles were not meant for publicity, to draw crowds, or to bring fame to Jesus. Often he wanted the miracles to be private and secret. Repeatedly he instructed healed persons, "Tell no man." (Mark 1:44) Since the Father gave the power to perform miracles to Jesus, the glory should be given to God alone.

2. To meet human need. Jesus performed miracles to relieve human suffering. He was motivated by compassion. When he saw a hungry multitude, out of compassion, he performed the miracle of the fish and loaves. When he saw a widow's only son on the way to a cemetery, he raised the young man because he felt sorry for the youth's mother. At Lazarus' grave, Jesus wept and then called him out of the tomb. His reason was expressed in Matthew's words, "His heart was filled with pity for them." (Matthew 9:36, GNB)

3. To announce the presence of the Kingdom of God. Through the miracles, Jesus showed that God's Kingdom was here. (Luke 11:20) By the power of God, demons were exorcised. God's power manifested in the miracles would cast down Satan. His marvelous works were meant to bring people to repentance. If the same miracles, he said, were done in the pagan cities, Tyre and Sidon, they would have repented. (Luke 10:13-15)

4. To proclaim truth. The miracles were an essential part of Jesus' ministry to proclaim the Word of God, the good news of salvation. This proclamation came through his words and deeds. His words were in parables; his deeds were in miracles. In his book, *Gravity and Grace,* Joseph Sittler said, "The parables are spoken miracles; the miracles are spoken parables." In each miracle there is a truth portrayed. These truths are "signs" pointing to a truth. The truth points to Christ as St. Augustine explains:

> *Let us ask of the miracles themselves what they will tell us about Christ; for if they be understood, they have a tongue of their own. He was the Word of God; and all the acts of the Word are themselves words for us; they are not as pictures, merely to look and admire, but as letters which we must seek to read and understand.*

Because of this purpose, we are justified in preaching the miracles for the truth enacted therein. A miracle has a message; each miracle has a tongue. As preachers, we must determine what the message is for today's people of God. Therefore, the significance of the miracles is more theological than historical. It is not merely a question of whether the miracle happened, but, more importantly, of what the miracle means for life today.

Faith and Miracles

What is the place of faith in miracles? Does faith create the miracle? Often Jesus said, "Your faith has made you well." (Mark 5:34) Will miracles happen if we have faith? Jesus said, "All things are possible to him who believes." (Mark 9:23) Because of the lack of faith, Jesus could not perform miracles in Nazareth. (Mark 6:5-6) In a religious periodical a writer wrote, "Without miracles, our faith cannot stand." Does our faith in Christ depend upon his miracles? No miracles, no faith?

Faith does not perform miracles. By the power of God, only Christ can do wondrous works. As R. C. Trench said many years ago, "We believe the miracles for Christ's sake." Faith allows God in Christ to perform the miracles. By faith we allow the miracles to happen to us. Faith does not come from the miracles; miracles come from faith.

In Jesus' miracles there is a variety of faith. At times no faith is expressed, but miracles happen. Peter's mother-in-law expressed no faith, but her fever was cured. During the storm at sea, the Disciples gave no indication of faith, but Jesus stilled the storm for them. At other times, faith is expressed by others than those healed. The Roman centurion had faith, but his servant did not. (Matthew 8:5-13) At the healing of the paralytic, Jesus saw the faith, not of the paralyzed man, but of the men who carried him to Jesus. (Matthew 9:1-7) Miracles were experienced by some who did not even know Jesus, such as the man healed at the pool of Bethesda (John 5:1-17) and the man born blind. (John 9:35-37)

This evidence shows us that Jesus' healing miracles were not what is popularly known as "faith healing." This is a form of psychosomatic healing. In some cases, there may have been a physical healing by a prior mental or spiritual healing. But Jesus healed whether

17

there was faith or no faith, whether there was faith on the part of the afflicted one or on the part of those who brought the patient.

Jesus and His Miracles

1. Classification of miracles
a. **Healings:** lepers, blind, crippled, paralyzed, et al.
b. **Exorcisms:** demons.
c. **Nature:** feeding thousands, stilling a storm, water to wine, et al.

2. Methods of healing.
a. **Healing by word only:** centurion's servant (Matthew 8:5-13)
b. **Healing by Jesus' touch:** Peter's mother-in-law (Matthew 8:15)
c. **Healing when Jesus was touched:** woman in a crowd (Mark 5:24-34)
d. **Healing by degrees:** blind man at Bethesda (Mark 8:22-26)
e. **Healing in absentia:** Syrophoenician woman's daughter (Mark 7:24-30)

Preaching the Miracles

1. What not to preach:
a. **Miracles are violations of natural laws.** Miracles only appear to violate the laws of nature. Miracles may occur by natural laws we do not understand or as yet are not discovered.
b. **Miracles are proofs of Jesus' deity.** Jesus is not God's Son or the Messiah because of his ability to perform miracles. People of the Bible, before and after Christ, performed miracles. This did not make them divine. Faith in Christ is not built upon Jesus' miracles. Rather, our faith is based on the Cross and Resurrection.
c. **Miracles are the work of Jesus.** Jesus' miracles are the work of God the Father, who worked in and through Jesus. Jesus did his wondrous works by virtue of the power of God's Spirit. To God be the glory for the miraculous work of his Son.
d. **Miracles are the result of faith only.** Jesus' miracles are not the result of faith healing. Jesus performed miracles when there was no faith expressed by those healed. His miracles are independent of human faith, although the lack of faith may prevent miracles from occurring to those who do not believe in Christ and his power to heal.

e. Miracles are the result of occult power. The Pharisees claimed that Jesus performed miracles by the power of Satan. He was accused of using black magic and occult power. He answered the charge by pointing out that if this were so, Satan's kingdom would be divided and could not stand. Jesus' miracles were the result of God's power — a positive, pure and holy power used only for good.

f. Miracles are examples of humanitarianism. The miracles are not examples to necessarily be imitated. They are not models of doing good or helping the hurting. Christians render aid to the sick and needy out of love for God as seen in Jesus.

2. What to preach:

a. The miracles are authentic. They really happened. They are neither myths nor legends.

b. The meaning of the miracle is to be preached. Though the historicity of the miracle is accepted, the spiritual and theological significance is far more important. The miracles tell us something important about Christ and life.

c. Preach not only what Jesus did in the past, but also what miracles he performs today.

d. Apply the message of the miracle to the needs, problems and questions of today's congregation. Let the miracle give its message to today's generation.

For Further Reading

Allen, Ronald J., *Our Eyes Can Be Opened*, University Press of America, 1982.

Barclay, William, *And He Had Compassion,* Judson, 1976.

Brown, Colin, *That You May Believe,* Eerdmanns, 1985.

Lewis, C. S., *Miracles,* Macmillan, 1947.

MacDonald, George, *The Miracles of Our Lord,* Howard Shaw Publishers, 1980.

Trench, R. C., *The Miracles of Our Lord,* Appleton, 1870.

Shut Up and Come Out!

Unclean Spirit   Mark 1:21-28 (Luke 4:31-37)

They went into Capernaum; and immediately on the sabbath he entered the syna-gogue and taught. ²²And they were astonished at his teaching, for he taught them as one who had authority, and not as the scribes. ²³And immediately there was in their synagogue a man with an unclean spirit; ²⁴and he cried out, "What have you to do with us, Jesus of Nazareth? Have you come to destroy us? I know who you are, the Holy One of God." ²⁵But Jesus rebuked him, saying, "Be silent, and come out of him!" ²⁶And the unclean spirit, convulsing him and crying with a loud voice, came out of him. ²⁷And they were all amazed, so that they questioned among themselves, saying, "What is this? A new teaching! With authority he commands even the unclean spirits, and they obey him." ²⁸And at once his fame spread every-where throughout all the surrounding region of Galilee.

    This is a true story of one claiming to be possessed of the devil. In the summer of 1988 at a northern camp meeting, a worshiper, after the evening service, said to the preacher, "I'm possessed of the devil. Do you think, if you prayed, that you could exorcise me of this evil spirit?"

    An appointment to discuss the concern was set for the next day. At this time she told her story, one of bitterness, anger and jealousy. She said she had been brought up in a Christian home, had an above average knowledge of the Bible, faithfully attended church services, and feared that her friends would learn of her possession. Though married, she admitted to two adulterous relationships.

    When she was asked why she thought she was possessed of an unclean spirit, she explained that several times a day, involuntarily, she would speak vile language and blasphemy against God. After a lengthy discussion, the preacher prayed with her, completed the laying on of hands, and prayed in Jesus' name. During the prayer, she clutched her throat and put her hand over her mouth to stop the deep gurgling caused by the evil spirit wanting to make her blaspheme. Finally, she begged the preacher to stop praying, saying that the devil was trying to get her to say all the foul, putrid obscenities contained within her. When she was assured that Jesus is stronger than the devil, she was asked if she believed in Jesus as God's Son. She nodded affirmatively. But, she could not bring herself to say, "Jesus Christ is Lord."

According to Mark, Jesus' first miracle involved a demon-possessed man in the Capernaum synagogue where Jesus was teaching. The unclean spirit caused the man to cry out against Jesus as the Holy One of God. With a few words, Jesus expelled the demon by commanding with authority, "Shut up and come out of him." Whether it is A.D. 30 or A.D. 2030, people are in need of a miracle to get free of an unclean spirit. Indeed, it is a miracle to get the devil out of you!

Acclimation

The Situation.

As Mark tells it, after Jesus' baptism and temptation, Jesus goes to Galilee where he calls two sets of brothers to be disciples: Peter and Andrew, James and John. Walking on the shore of the Sea of Galilee, he comes to Capernaum, where on a sabbath he teaches. The congregation is impressed because his teaching is different from the teaching of the scribes, the Biblical scholars of their day. He teaches as one with firsthand authority. His teaching is interrupted by a man's screams. The man yells, "What do you have to do with us?" An evil spirit makes him say this. Yes, what does a holy spirit have to do with an evil spirit? Can oil and water mix? The unclean spirit is referred to as "us," even though there is only one man who screams. (Apparently, evil spirits sometimes come in bunches. In another case of a man with an unclean spirit, when Jesus asked him his name, he said his name was "Legion," for he was many. [Mark 5:9]) The evil spirit recognizes Jesus as the Messiah, "The Holy One of God." What the people do not see in Jesus, the unclean spirit does. With an authoritarian voice, Jesus orders the evil spirit to be silent and to leave the man. Apparently, it does, because the people are astonished at the results. Earlier they were impressed by his authoritative teaching; but now they are amazed that his authority can free a person from demon possession. As a result, his fame as a teacher and healer spreads throughout Galilee.

The Setting.

1. The Church Year. The miracle of Jesus' driving out an evil spirit is the Gospel for the Fourth Sunday after the Epiphany. The Epiphany season consists of eight Sundays between the Festival of the Epiphany (the visit of the Wise Men) and the Transfiguration. Seven of the eight gospels are taken from the first two chapters of Mark. The miracle fits into the theme of the Epiphany season, which deals with the manifestation of the glory of God in Jesus. In the miracle, God's glory can be seen in Jesus' authority to exorcise evil spirits simply by word of command.

2. Parallel Passage: (Luke 4:31-37). The account of the miracle is given by Luke also. The two stories are almost identical. Mark refers to the "unclean spirit" (v. 23); Luke calls it an "unclean demon." (v. 33) Both refer to Jesus' authority in teaching, but Mark contrasts it with that of the teachers of the day — "not as the scribes." (v. 22) In Mark the evil spirit "came out of him" (v. 26), but Luke assures us that despite the violent convulsions, there was no harm done to the man: "having done him no harm." (v. 35) In Mark the people say, "With authority he commands" (v. 27), but Luke reports, "with authority and power he commands." The Greek word, exousia, means authority or power or both. Both are inter-related because authority without power is helpless, and power without authority is lawlessness. Jesus had authority and power from his Father.

3. The Lectionary. During the Epiphany season, the Lessons do not necessarily point toward a common theme. However, it may be possible to see a connection of the gospel with the First and Second Lessons.

Lesson 1: Deuteronomy 18:15-20. God promises to raise up a prophet like Moses who will speak the words of God. This promise is fulfilled in Jesus who speaks God's Word. This is shown in the Gospel by his word's driving out an unclean spirit with the authority and power of God's Word.

Lesson 2: 1 Corinthians 8:1-13. The passage deals with food offered to idols. The idols are like the unclean spirits of the possessed man in today's miracle. There is but one God, one Holy Spirit. Other spirits are not of God.

Gospel: Mark 1:21-28. According to Mark, Jesus begins his ministry at Capernaum by driving out an unclean spirit. In the remaining Sundays after the Epiphany, three additional miracles occur. They witness to the glory of God in Jesus' ministry.

Explanation

Capernaum (v. 21).

Today, Capernaum, once located on the Sea of Galilee, is known as "The Town of Jesus." It was the base of his Galilean ministry. It was also the home town of Peter and Andrew. Since it was a tax station, probably it was in Capernaum that Jesus called Matthew, a tax collector. It is mentioned thirty-seven times in the New Testament, more often than any other town. Today, Capernaum no longer exists, but ruins of a synagogue can still be seen: the foundation stones and sections of the walls. A nearby Franciscan monastery serves as caretaker of the sacred ground upon which the synagogue is built.

Synagogue (v. 21).

A synagogue is a meeting place for the Jews. It came into existence during the Babylonian exile as a substitute for the Jerusalem temple destroyed in 586 B.C. It was a place for instruction in the Law and the Prophets. The Torah was divided into 155 sections so that in three years the entire law was read. After the lection for the day was read, an exposition of the passage followed. A visiting teacher could be invited to give the exposition as Jesus did at Capernaum. The invitation was extended by the ruler of the synagogue, who was responsible for law and order in the assembly. The chief piece of furniture was the ark, or shrine, in which the sacred scrolls were kept. In addition, there was an elevated wooden pulpit, similar to the one used by Ezra (Nehemiah 8:4-5) for the reading. The speaker was usually seated while addressing the worshipers. As was his custom, this sabbath Jesus went to synagogue and this time was invited to speak. During his teaching, he was interrupted by a man's screaming. This resulted in today's miracle.

Scribes (v. 22).

The scribes in Jesus' day were scholars of the Mosaic law. Because of their knowledge and dealings with the law, they were sometimes called "lawyers," as we today call those who are experts in the law. The scribes had an authority different from that of Jesus. Their authority came from the written scrolls and the respected commentators on the law. Jesus' authority was different because he *was* the authority for what he taught. He could say, "But I say to you." (Matthew 5:28) Since he was the "Holy One of God," he had the direct authority of God. It was the difference between human and divine authority. Consequently, the authoritative teaching of Jesus was astonishing for the synagogue hearers.

Unclean Spirit (v. 23).

Unclean spirit, demon, and devil are used interchangeably. In the parallel account (Luke 4:33), it is translated: "a man who had the spirit of an unclean demon." Later in Mark's first chapter, we are told that Jesus "cast out many devils." (v. 34) The Revised Standard Version and the Good News Bible use "demons" rather than "devils."

An unclean spirit is the opposite of the Holy Spirit. Demons are unclean spirits allied with the devil, Satan. It was believed that the unclean spirits caused physical and mental illnesses. The demons were associated with darkness, destruction and death.

The Jews used various devices to scare off demons: 1. Bells were placed on the robe of the high priest for entering the holy of holies; 2. Bells were rung. In some churches today, a bell is tolled when the Lord's Prayer is prayed; 3. A ram's horn was blown; 4. Blood was placed on doorposts and lintels; 5. A blue cord was placed on the hem of one's garment (Numbers 15:38); 6. Wearing the Torah on the hand and in frontlets.

Holy One of God (v. 24).

"Holy one of Israel" was a title of Yahweh. In the New Testament it is applied to the Messiah as in verse 24 and Acts 3;14 and 2 John 2:20. The unclean spirit in the worshiper recognized Jesus as the very Son of God, the promised Messiah. Is it not strange that the demons knew the identity of Jesus when the faithful failed to see who he really was?

Application

Relevance of Revelation.

Before we can preach on this miracle, we must be convinced of its relevance to today's life situation. Is there a need for a sermon on this miracle? Is it a vital need? Is it important enough to merit the time and effort?

The miracle deals primarily with authority. People were impressed with the authority of Jesus' teachings and with his authority over evil powers. What place does authority have in the 1990s? Since the '60's, there has been an erosion in authority. For some, the Bible is no longer an authority as God's Word. In the classroom, the teacher is no longer respected as one with authority. Many Roman Catholics reject the authority of the Vatican in matters of sexual ethics. One of today's most influential books on preaching is entitled *As One without Authority*. Our expanding crime rate expresses our current lack of authority in law and order. There is a general revulsion against authority in terms of authoritarianism, which comes across as dogmatism, dictatorship, and submission. On the other hand, people feel the need of true authority as Jesus expressed it. They want a sure and certain word for these times of turbulence and confusion. The question is whether we can have *authority* without *authoritarianism*. Can we preach with authority without coming across as authoritarian?

The miracle for this Sunday deals specifically with Jesus' authority over unclean spirits. Before we can deal with this subject in preaching, we need to think through our stand on evil spirits, demons, and the devil. Today, many deny the reality or at least minimize the reality of evil powers. Professor Temba Mafico of Zimbabwe said in reference to demons: "It is real to Africans, at least they believe it is real, so we must treat it as though it is real even though we do not personally accept it as real." Can we preach dynamically and effectively on this miracle of cleansing a person of an unclean spirit if we just make believe it is true? Is the idea of a demon-possessed person an ancient, pre-scientific superstition? Is an unclean spirit really only a symptom of mental illness?

For Jesus, the devil with his power of evil was a reality. In the wilderness he confronted Satan for forty days. He promised that "the powers of death" would not destroy his church. At Caesarea Philippi he acknowledged the presence of Satan in Peter. In this and other miracles by the finger of God he cast out satanic forces.

For Paul, evil was a reality that possessed people. To the Ephesians Paul wrote: "We are not contending against flesh and blood, but against the principalities against the powers, against the rulers of this present darkness, against the spiritual hosts of wickedness in heavenly places." (6:12)

For Luther, Satan with his powers working in people, was a reality. In "A Mighty Fortress, he has us sing about Satan:

> And though this world, with devils filled,
> Should threaten to undo us;
> We will not fear, for God hath willed
> His truth to triumph through us.
> The prince of darkness grim,
> We tremble not for him;
> His rage we can endure,
> For lo! his doom is sure
> One little word shall fell him.

How can one explain the terrible, horrible crimes in our society, from senseless murder to mutilation to torture to genocide? How does one explain a dastardly deed like Judas' betrayal? John had the explanation: "Satan entered into him." (John 13:27) For us today, can there be any better explanation? Evil spirits in people cause them to do horrible deeds. Can we preach on this miracle with integrity? The answer is *yes*. Satan *is* real. He does possess people in terms of unclean spirits. We can be demon possessed to the extent that an evil spirit has captured us. The good news we have to preach is that Jesus is the solution to demon possession. He alone has the authority to say to an evil spirit, "Come out of him." (Mark 1:25)

Sermon Suggestions.

1. People Who Should Know Don't. Why did the possessed man in the miracle recognize the true identity of Jesus when the devout people in the synagogue did not? The man screamed, "I know who you are, the Holy One of God." (v. 24) He saw the Messiah in Jesus. The people heard only a good teacher and a miracle worker. They had no confession such as "You are the Christ, the Son of the living God." John the Baptizer could have said to them, "Among you stands one whom you do not know." (John 1:26) Is it the same with church people today? Do they not see the Christ in Jesus? Do they see only a teacher, a prophet, or a healer? Would Jesus ask today's disciples the same question he asked of the Twelve, "Who do you say that I am?"

2. Friend or Foe? "Have you come to destroy us?" asked the unclean spirit. Here we have a confrontation between good and evil, between Christ and Satan. They cannot compromise nor co-exist. One or the other will be destroyed. On Good Friday Satan thought

26

he had destroyed his enemy, but God the Father fooled him. Thus, on Easter we sing, "The strife is o'er, the battle's won. Alleluia!" Evil cannot bear the presence of good. The Spirit of God scatters evil spirits. On the external walls of Gothic cathedrals, you can see gargoyles which are horrible, ferocious, Satanic figures. They represent demons fleeing from the presence of God within the church. This miracle demonstrates the good news that the power of God is far greater than the power of Satan.

3. *No Rest for the Wicked.* The exit of the unclean spirit was violent. As it left the man, it caused convulsions and made him scream. Evil and violence are roommates. There is no rest for the wicked. An evil spirit calls for burn, blast, destroy, and kill. A fruit of the Holy Spirit is peace. Christ with the Holy Spirit was a man of peace and refused to use force even for self-preservation. Terrorism, murder, rape, abuse are the work of an unclean spirit. Obviously, the solution to bombings and bloodshed is persuading people to have a good spirit in their hearts.

4. *An Interrupted Lesson.* All seemed to be going well as Jesus taught in the synagogue. It was so quiet that you could hear a pin drop, because what he said was very interesting, spell-binding, and authoritative. All of a sudden there was a piercing scream. A heckler was in the congregation. The people were shocked and turned to look at the disturber of the peace and interrupter of the finest speech they had ever heard. Why did this man cry out? Because Jesus was speaking truth, and the demon could not tolerate it. Falsehood cannot share the same bed with truth. Sin cannot mix with holiness. No one can have it both ways: it's either God's or Satan's way.

5. *One Little Word.* Jesus' words had authority because they came out of the mouth of God. His words also had power. To exorcise the unclean spirit, Jesus only said, "Be silent and come out of him!" No sooner said than done! Jesus did not use magic, call down angels, or use mumbo-jumbo incantations. He used only simple words. This is possible because God's Word is linked with God's Spirit, which is the power of God. The Word changes things, performs miracles, and transforms lives. Speaking of Satan, Luther sang, "One little word shall fell him."

6. *An Unwanted Confession.* If Jesus is the "Holy One of God" and the possessed man confessed it before the whole congregation, why did Jesus command, "Be silent!"? At other times Jesus told ones he healed that they should tell no one. Could it be that Jesus

wanted the people to find out for themselves? Jesus did not even tell his Disciples who he really was. He asked them, "Who do you say that I am?" Jesus wanted the people to come to their own conclusions, as the centurion at the Cross did when he confessed, "Truly this man was a son of God." (Mark 15:39) If we come to our own conclusions based on what we have heard and seen, we are convinced that he is the Christ.

7. *Not What, but How.* The account of the miracle tells us that Jesus was teaching, but it does not tell what he taught. The people were astonished not at the content, but at the method. It was one of authority. Indeed, what he taught was the truth of God, which called people to repent and believe. They may have heard this before from John the Baptizer. But Jesus' method was different from the scribes because he taught with confidence, conviction, and sincerity. He knew what he was talking about. This should not surprise us, for Biblical scholars tell us that what Jesus taught had been, for the most part, taught before. It is not what you say, but how you say it. The how describes your spirit, attitude, integrity and sincerity.

8. *Bad in the Best of Us.* It is said that there is good in the worst of us. It can also be said that there is bad in the best of us. Consider the man upon whom the miracle was performed. He was in the synagogue praying, worshiping and listening to God's Word read and taught. He was obedient to God's law: "Remember the sabbath day to keep it holy." He was in the good company of God's people. Nothing is said of his having any doubts or whether he lived immorally. We assume he was an honest and upright man. But, it was this man who was so possessed of the devil that he screamed and shook with convulsions. It reminds us that Satan can dwell in church people. Christians are both saints and sinners simultaneously. Church people live in a constant tension caused by good and evil spirits in their hearts. The unclean spirit must ever be renounced and a fresh supply of the Holy Spirit prayed for to counteract the evil spirit.

Sermon Structures.

1. Victory in Jesus (vv. 21-28). If an unclean spirit possesses us, how can we get it out of us? Can Jesus relieve us of a bad spirit just as he exorcised the demon from the man in the miracle? Jesus is still alive and is concerned about our well-being. He can give us victory over unclean spirits.

A. Use the name of Jesus — v. 24
B. Speak the Word of God in Jesus — v. 25
C. Possess the Spirit of Jesus — 1 John 4:4
D. Put on the armor of God — Ephesians 6:10-17

2. The Truth about Demons (vv. 23-26). In our sophisticated and scientific age, some people may consider evil spirits a superstition from the Dark Ages. If one is possessed, we may think the person needs a therapist or psychiatrist rather than a pastor. In contrast, the greatest Christians — Jesus, Paul, Peter — believed in and dealt with demons. This miracle calls our attention to these facts:

A. Evil spirits (demons) are real — v. 23
B. Evil spirits can possess a human — v. 23
C. Evil spirits can be removed — vv. 25, 26

3. As One with Authority (vv. 21-28). Today's Gospel Lesson points to the authority of Jesus expressed in word (teaching) and in deed (exorcism). Where did he get his authority?

A. Jesus had the authority of God's Son — v. 24 (An inherent authority based on his identity.)
B. Jesus had the authority of God's Word — v. 25 (See John 12:49)
C. Jesus demonstrated his authority — vv. 25, 26

4. The Message of the Miracle (vv. 21-28). A miracle is an enacted parable. A miracle can speak. What is the miracle saying to us?

A. Evil is a reality — v. 23
B. The church consists of sinners as well as saints — v. 23
C. Christ can evict an evil spirit — v. 25

5. You Can Have Authority (vv. 22, 27). A Christian can have authority as the Master had. You can be confident and certain. It is not necessary to suppose or guess or conjecture. You can speak and act with assurance. With Luther, you can say, "This is most certainly true." Christians know who they are, where they stand, and what they believe. A true Christian is not a wimp or a milquetoast. A Christian can have authority.

A. So long as a Christian speaks God's Word.
With authority one can say, "Except you repent, you will perish," or "Believe in Jesus and you will be saved," or "Because of your faith, you will go to heaven."

B. So long as a Christian possesses the spirit of Christ.
The spirit of Christ has the power of the Holy Spirit. With the Spirit, one can authoritatively speak to the unsaved and help the helpless. This is done with confidence and assurance of doing the right thing.

Illustration

Troubled Minds.

The National Institute of Mental Health reported in 1988 the results of an eight-year survey of 18,571 adults: fifteen percent suffered anxiety disorders; eight percent experienced major depression; one of every six has been dependent on drugs or alcohol; one-third of all Americans suffer from an acute mental illness at some point in their lives.

How You Say It.

A cartoon showed two men manacled to a wall. The one said to the other, "It wasn't so much what I said. It was the way I said it."

Death and the Devil.

In 1415 John Huss was burned at the stake. Before the fire started, his enemies placed a crown of paper painted with devils on his head. Huss responded: "My Lord, Jesus Christ, for my sake, wore a crown of thorns; why should not I then, for His sake, wear this light crown, be it ever so ignominious? Truly, I will do it willingly."

Power and Authority.

The difference between authority and power: Power is the ability to effect one's ends or purposes in the world. Authority is not only having power but the *right* to use it to reach one's purpose.

Evidence of Today's Unclean Spirits.

Pornography: it is an eight-billion-dollar industry in the United States. Twenty million magazines are published each month. Books are entitled: *Anal Games with my Sister, I Took my Bra off for Daddy, A Manuel for Rape,* and *Lust for Fun.*

Hard Rock Music: The average teenager listens to rock music four hours a day. A lyric: "We're possessed by all that is evil; the death of you, God, we demand. We spit at the virgin you worship, and sit at Lord Satan's left hand." It has been estimated that obscene material is found in one-third of all rock releases. Rock music extols everything from rape and incest to bestiality. The lyrics often glamorize drugs, alcohol, death, violence and suicide.

Astrology: horoscopes appear daily in 2,000 American newspapers. Thirty-two million Americans believe in astrology and spend one billion dollars annually for astrological materials and services. In May 1988 the news media reported that Nancy Reagan consulted an astrologer for dates when the President could safely travel.

Fortune telling: Two women, Helene and Helena, convinced a husband and wife that they were possessed by evil. To rid themselves of evil, the couple paid $32,000 in cash.

Demons.

Ruth Seamands' book, *Pearls in the Rain* is set in New Guinea. The natives are plagued with fears: evil spirits, witch doctors and enemies who put the devil on them. Mance, a New Guinea native, was very sick. Her minister said, "She will probably die because another woman put the devil on her. The other woman thinks that Mance is trying to get her husband." She told Mance that the devil would come and get her in three days. It was now the third day and Mance was waiting to die. A missionary went into her room and found her terrified with her eyes rolling. He placed his hand on her head, closed his eyes, and prayed. Then he said, "Mance, I command the devil in Jesus' name not to come near you at all. Not ever! Your life is not over, for God has work for you to do." Then in a strong commanding voice he said, "Now, Mance, get up out of bed and go pay attention only to your own husband! Pray and work and behave yourself. Then the devil cannot harm you." Then Mance got off the bed, got her hoe and started digging sweet potatoes for her family's supper. She was never sick a day since that time.

Satanism.

In September 1987, on a Sunday afternoon in a Bible Belt town of 4,000 located in Missouri, three teenage boys beat to death a friend with seventy slugs from baseball bats. They had become involved in Satanism and used the friend as a sacrifice. The leader explained, "I was fascinated by death. I always had this obsession with killing things. I don't know really what it was. Like when I started out as a little kid, I couldn't shoot a bird and watch it die. I had to tear it up." The three youths received life sentences without parole. Jim, their leader, wrote a letter from jail admitting that Satan had tricked them and said, "I don't even know why we killed Steve. It was like any other animal we killed."

Knowing a Name.

There is a classic story about a miller's daughter who had to spin straw into gold to marry the king. She was about to give up on this impossible task when a little man approached her and offered to spin the straw into gold on condition that she would give him her first son. She agreed to the bargain. The straw was spun into gold and the girl married the king. When the son was born, the little man returned and demanded that she give him the child. She offered him all of her wealth, but he refused. He insisted upon having the baby. Seeing how difficult it was for her, the little man made another proposal. If she could give him his name, she could keep the baby. For days she searched the royal library, but her efforts were in vain. Then a messenger gave her a report of a strange sight he had seen. One night on a high hill he had witnessed a little man dancing around a fire singing: "Oh, little thinks my royal dame, that Rumpelstiltskin is my name." When the little man came to the Queen the next day, she told him that his name was Rumpelstiltskin. Then he screamed, "The devil it is, the devil it is!" He stamped his foot on the ground so forcefully that he split himself in two.

A House Healing

A Mother-in-law
sick in bed
with a fever

Mark 1:29-31
(Matthew 8:14-15;
Luke 4:38-39)

Epiphany 5

29Immediately he left the synagogue, and entered the house of Simon and Andrew, with James and John. 30Now Simon's mother-in-law lay sick with a fever, and immediately they told him of her. 31And he came and took her by the hand and lifted her up, and the fever left her; and she served them.

Peter's house in which, according to Mark, Jesus performed his first physical healing, has recently (1988) been discovered by archaeologists. This house is believed to be Peter's home in Capernaum where Jesus stayed, taught and healed. The discovery has been substantiated by James H. Charlesworth, a professor at Princeton Theological Seminary, in his book, *Jesus Within Judaism.*

The house is dated at 60 B.C. It contains Greek, Aramaic, Syriac, Latin and Hebrew graffiti done by second-and-third-century Christians. Also, the house contains crosses etched on walls, a boat, ritualistic pottery and, between floor boards, a number of fish hooks indicating that the occupant was a fisherman.

This house is the scene of this Sunday's miracle: the healing of Peter's mother-in-law, who was sick in bed with a fever. It was a small beginning of Jesus' healing physical ailments, but it led to big things before the day was over. It was held in the privacy of a home with only a few friends present. It was not a serious illness, for in a few days with proper rest and diet, she probably would have recovered. The illness could not be compared with leprosy or blindness. Though it was a minimal miracle, it still has much to say about Jesus in his concern for the slightest illness of an ordinary person. Who has not had at some time a high temperature? There is no problem or illness too small for Jesus' healing mercy. The little miracle must have been important to the early church, for all three Synoptic writers record the incident.

33

Acclimation

The Situation.

Jesus goes from his first healing of a mental illness according to Mark, to his first physical healing. The teaching and healing in the Capernaum synagogue met with great success; the people were amazed at his authority and power. Now the sabbath service is over and it is time for the noonday meal. Where is Jesus to go? He has no home and no one to prepare a meal for him. Peter is kind enough to say, "Come to my house and we'll get something to eat." With Andrew, James and John, Peter and Jesus go to his home. When they get settled, Jesus finds that not all is well. Peter's mother-in-law is in bed sick with a high fever. At once he goes to her, offers her his hand, and helps her to get up. At once the fever leaves her and she returns to the kitchen to serve the men a meal.

The Setting.

1. The Pericope (Mark 1:29-39). The miracle is contained in a passage of ten verses. It tells us of Jesus' first physical healing. (vv. 29-31) This opens the flood gates for the sick of the town to flock to Peter's home for Jesus to heal them. Because of the sabbath law prohibiting the carrying of burdens, the people wait until sundown, the end of the sabbath day. The news of the first healing spreads like wildfire as though blown by a Santa Ana wind in California, and all the sick appear. Jesus heals many of them. He is so busy that he has no time for himself or to pray. Early the next morning while others are alseep, he goes outside the village to a lonely spot to be alone with God. Peter leads a hunting party and finds him and tells him that "Everyone is searching for you." Jesus does not return to Capernaum, but goes to other towns to preach and heal. He sees his mission not as one limited to a locality, but as one open to the whole nation.

2. Parallel Accounts: Matthew 8:14-15; Luke 4:38-39. Slight *differences* in the accounts:

a. Fever — in Mark and Matthew the woman is "sick with fever" but Luke calls it a "high fever."

b. Method of cure — *Matthew:* "Touched her hand and the fever left her, and she arose and served him." Here the healing results from Jesus' touch and then the woman gets up on her own strength.

Mark: "Took her by the hand and lifted her up, and the fever left her." In this case, Jesus lifted the woman out of bed by taking her hand.

Luke: "They besought him for her"; "He stood over her and rebuked the fever, and it left her." According to Luke, Jesus was asked by the men to heal the woman. He did not touch her. Rather he rebuked the fever as though it were a demon, and the fever left her.

c. Service — Mark and Luke say that the healed woman "served him," just Jesus. Matthew reports that she served "them," the five men and others who may have been there.

Agreement in the passages:

a. Jesus entered Peter's home for dinner
b. Peter's mother-in-law was sick with a fever.
c. Jesus healed her of the fever.
d. The mother-in-law responded with service.

3. The Lectionary.

Lesson 1 (Job 7:1-7). Job describes his miserable condition; he feels hopeless with nothing to live for, physically in pain from sores, and extremely unhappy. The relation to today's miracle: Job needs a miracle of healing as do many in Capernaum who are physically and mentally ill. Like the mother-in-law, Job is suffering with a fever of the heart as well as the body.

Lesson 2 (1 Corinthians 9:16-23). In order to win people to faith in the Gospel, Paul identifies with all sorts of people — those under and not under the Law, and the weak. He preaches not for a reward but out of inner necessity resulting from his commission to preach. The relation to the miracle: As Jesus dealt with a "nobody" with a fever, Paul deals with the lowest as well as the highest of people. As the healed woman did not ask for a reward for serving the meal, Paul does not preach for a reward, but preaches out of an inner call. Like Paul, Jesus is a man for all people.

Gospel (Mark 1:29-39). Wherever Jesus goes, there is a hurting person. In the synagogue a demon-possessed man screams. After the service, Jesus goes to a home for dinner. There he finds a physically ill person. His success in curing the woman results in a crowd of sick people begging for help. In the midst of helping people, he feels the need to go to the source of his power and authority, his heavenly Father. He goes to a solitary place to get help from God that he might help others.

Explanation

Mother-in-law (v. 30).

We are not given her name. She is known only in association with Peter, for she was his mother-in-law. Since her daughter was an adult, we can assume that she was an old woman. Moreover, because she lived with Peter and her daughter, she must have been widowed and poor. Yet, she was useful and helped with the housework.

If Peter had a mother-in-law, he also had a wife. Paul makes mention in his Corinthians letter of Peter's taking his wife with him on his missionary trips. (1 Corinthians 9:5) If, as the Roman Church claims, Peter founded the church at Rome and was the first pope, how could he be married when the Roman Church requires celibacy for the priesthood? Celibacy was introduced by Pope Gregory VII in the eleventh century. For the previous thousand years, priests had had families. A great divorce came when priests were required to get rid of their wives. Celibacy, the pope claimed, was necessary because a priest is married to the Church. Celibacy is a more holy way of life, and more pleasing to God. In recent years a movement in the Roman Church attempts to return to Peter's status and thus to permit priests to marry. If marriage was good and holy enough for St. Peter, why would it not be good for priests in the twenty-first century?

Fever (v. 30).

The nature of the mother-in-law's fever is not known. Was it a common low or a high fever? Some think it was the result of a common cold. Or, it may have been caused by typhus. The most popular view is that it was caused by malaria, for in Capernaum and Tiberias malaria was quite prevalent. In the Old Testament a fever is considered to be a curse resulting from breaking the covenant with God. (Deuteronomy 28:22) Consequently, it was allied with Satan. Perhaps that was Luke's understanding of it, for he reports that Jesus rebuked the fever as he had rebuked Satan.

Lifted (v. 31).

Without saying a word, according to Mark, Jesus went into the woman's bedroom and found her in bed with a high fever. He reached out his hand to take hers and then he lifted her up or, as we say, pulled her up. It was better than a word. It was a personal touch. Power apparently went out of him and entered her so that her fever was gone. In the Talmud "lift up" was a term used for curing or healing. The woman was in the depth of illness and pain, and Jesus lifted her to health and well-being.

Served (v. 31).

The fact that she served Jesus and his friends a meal indicates that though it was a slight miracle, it was speedy. She needed no time to rest or get her bearings. She was up and at the job in no time! According to Jewish custom, the main sabbath meal was served right after the synagogue service. Thus, Jesus and his friends probably gathered at a table while the mother-in-law served their food. It was unusual for her to be allowed to serve, because the rabbis objected to a woman serving at tables. For them it had to be waiters, not waitresses!

Application

The Relevance of Revelation.

Does this little miracle of curing a fever in a mother-in-law have anything to say to people about to enter the twenty-first century? Is there a revelation of truth in the miracle? If so, what is its relevance?

First, the miracle relates to today's homes and homelessness. Jesus had no home. He entered a friend's home where he was given something to eat and a place to rest. Today the home is in a desperate situation. Millions of people are homeless. They sleep on the streets and eat at soup kitchens. Half of our homes are disintegrating through divorce and separation. Single parents are numerous. A majority of homes still intact are reported to house unhappy mates.

Next, this miracle is relevant to our life situations not only in that our homes are sick, but also in that illness of body, mind or emotions prevails in almost every home. Jesus did not suspect that a sick person was in Peter's home. We, too, will find that almost every family has some problem or need. Practically every person has some hurt, large or small. Today we are in desperate need of healing.

Also, Jesus came into Peter's house by invitation. Many homes today need the presence of Jesus. His absence is seen in the lack of family devotions, the disappearance of the family pew, overpermissive parents and hostility expressed in spouse and child abuse. When Jesus is invited into a home, he makes a tremendous difference through healing, peace and joy.

Sermon Suggestions.

1. Home Healing. The miracle took place in Peter's home. In it there was a sick member of the family. Today our homes are on the sick list. Members of the family need healing because in many homes there are strife, discord, misunderstanding, as well as possible physical illness. The illness takes the form of adultery, rape, spouse and child abuse. What or who can save our homes from dissolution? Christ in the home is the only answer. For Christ to come into the home, he must first come by invitation into the hearts of the members of the family.

2. The Grace of Hospitality. Since Jesus had no home or family in Capernaum, he had nowhere to go, no place to get dinner. Peter had the grace to ask Jesus to come home with him for a meal. It is a grace that is fast disappearing today. Seldom are we invited to a home for a meal. If friends today want to share a meal, they usually go to a restaurant and each family "goes dutch." Jesus will not come into our homes unless he is invited. Think of the rewards of that invitation: the charming presence of Jesus at your table and a healing to boot!

3. Healed to Help. Today people are in search of the meaning of life. What is life all about? Why am I here on earth? Death seems to make life meaningless. It makes us leave everything we worked for. At death our knowledge and skills evaporate. The miracle gives us a clue to life's meaning. The healed woman immediately began to serve Jesus and his friends. "She served them." (v. 31) We are here to serve, to help, to do good and to build a better world. Even Jesus understood that his life was "not to be served but to serve." Service is a normal response in terms of gratitude for the healing, the blessings received from Christ.

4. A Borrowed Home. The birds have nests, the foxes have holes, but Jesus had no place to lay his head. Peter's home was a borrowed home for Jesus. Even when he was born, there was no room in anyone's home. As a refugee in Egypt, the holy family had no home. Praise and thanks to Peter for giving Jesus a home that day! It reminds us of the millions of people in America and throughout the world who have no homes. The homeless sleep in cars, on park benches and in gutters. Even more, we need a spiritual home, a church home and a heavenly home.

5. *An Uplift.* The story of the miracle tells us how Jesus healed the woman of her fever. He gave her his hand "and lifted her up." (v. 31) This is what Jesus will do for all of us who are down and out. Many women, like the mother-in-law, need to be lifted up to dignity and equality with men. All of us need an uplift from despair to hope, from hatred to love, from death to life. Tragically, many today try to get this high by drugs, alcohol and sex. These result in further depth and in an early death. Christ can lift us up to new heights of living.

6. *Tell it to Jesus.* When Jesus came into Peter's home, "they told" about the sick mother-in-law. If they had not told him, he probably would not have known of her illness. Pastors often say, "How can I visit you in the hospital if I am not told about it?" That is the purpose of prayer. We tell Jesus about our and others' needs. A hymn says, "Take it to the Lord in prayer." The miracle assures us that when Jesus knows of our condition, he comes and helps us.

7. *A Wordless Miracle.* This is a strange miracle in that it is wordless. Mark does not record a word spoken by Jesus and not a word from the woman. It is entirely communication by body language: "hand," "lifted," "served." Non-verbal language is a more effective means of communication than is speech. A picture is better than a verbal description. An act or life says more than talk. "I'd rather see a sermon than hear one any day." By his act, Jesus showed his concern, willingness and power to help a sick woman. The healed woman spoke her gratitude through her service. Who you are and what you do tells the world what master you follow.

8. *The Least.* Compared with other miracles, this one is not very spectacular. It was performed in the privacy of a home. The problem was relatively minor — just a high temperature. The woman was old and a mother-in-law. In Jesus' day women were little more than a man's property. Mothers-in-law are often disparaged by unkind mother-in-law jokes and wisecracks. Yet, she was an important person with value and dignity so far as Jesus was concerned. He had compassion for the least of people. That includes you and me!

Sermon Structures.

1. *The Gospel in a Miracle (vv. 29-31).* Where is the Gospel in this miracle? What does it have to say about our salvation? The

danger of a miracle is that we overlook the message in favor of the method.

A. Christ is concerned about our welfare — "He came"

B. Christ is able to help us — "lifted her up"

C. Christ ministers to the least of us — "Simon's mother-in-law"

2. A Miracle for Common People (vv. 29-31). There was nothing unusual or spectacular about this miracle. It is a miracle for an ordinary person with an ordinary ailment.

A. A common person: an aged woman, mother-in-law

B. A common ailment: fever

C. A common responsibility: wait on table, serve

D. A common miracle: one of many that day — v. 34

3. A Wordless Miracle (vv. 29-31). Here is a body language miracle. No word was spoken except Peter's telling of the presence of a sick woman. The point is that by body language we communicate probably more effectively than by words.

A. No word from the woman — fever was a message of need.

B. No word from Jesus — lifting her was a message of compassion

C. No word from the Disciples — their response brought the town's sick to Jesus

4. A Lift for Your Life (vv. 29-31). Today many turn to drugs, alcohol or sex to get a lift out of the doldrums to ecstacy. Jesus lifted the woman from sickness to health. Jesus will do the same today:

A. From sickness to health

B. From despair to hope

C. From sin to salvation

D. From death to life

5. A Reason to Live (vv. 29-31). A basic problem today for many is to find the meaning of life. A fundamental reason to live is to serve. The healed woman immediately began to serve by preparing a meal. "She served him." (v. 31) The purpose of life is to serve Christ and people for Jesus' sake. This was the purpose of Jesus' life: not to be served, but to serve.

A. Service — the purpose of life

B. Service — the motivation: gratitude

C. Service — the reward: knowledge of doing God's will

6. Healed to Help (vv. 29-31). In this sermon let's be practical, especially so! Tell the "how" of service. Be specific and concrete

40

with regard to the daily life of a parishioner. How can we today serve Christ?

A. Help others in need — "Inasmuch as you have done it to one of these . . ."

B. Give donations — share our money

C. Daily work — vocation done to God's glory

D. Church — teaching, visiting, singing, ushering, etc.

Illustration

The Homeless.

One out of four persons in the world either is homeless or lives under wretched and unhealthy conditions. According to the United Nations, 100 million people sleep in the streets, under bridges, in gateways or on deserted property. The United States has two-and-a-half million homeless people.

The Least of These.

"For want of a nail the shoe was lost. For want of a shoe the horse was lost. For want of a horse the rider was lost. For want of a rider the kingdom was lost and all for the want of a horseshoe nail!"

Uplift.

A trainer of seeing-eye dogs for the blind says that the most difficult thing in training dogs for the blind is to lift the eye level of the dog. The eye level of a dog is about eighteen inches above the ground; the eye level of a human is five feet or more above the ground. Consequently, an obstruction crossing the path of a blind person at the height of four to six feet is not an obstruction for the dog. So the dog's eye level must be lifted for it to see what a person would see. "I will life up my eyes to the Lord." "Seek that which is above."

A Life of Service.

In his lifetime John Wesley, founder of Methodism, travelled 250,000 miles on horseback, preached 1,000 times per year, wrote 400 books and established hundreds of societies, schools, hospitals and orphanages.

Getting High.

A nineteen-year-old youth of Hastings, Nebraska was recently arrested for possession of forty-nine capsules of the psychoactive drug, Ecstasy.

Service through the Church.

Churches devote nearly half of the money that they receive to charity. The study was made from May 1987 through March 1988 by Independent Sector, which represents 650 foundations and organizations. Nineteen point one billion dollars of the forty-one point four billion dollars contributed in 1986 to congregations was used for service to others. Volunteer work by the members of the congregation was valued at thirteen billion dollars. The survey showed that nine out of ten congregations had at least one program in human services and welfare.

No Room.

A prayer by Joseph Bayly:

> *Lord, we blame the innkeeper for only giving you the stable when his inn was full but what about all the others who lived in Bethlehem that night when you were born? Why were all their houses that weren't full of guests fast closed against the one who contained you? God bless our little homes this Christmastime. Make them big enough to welcome you contained in those for whom the world has no room except a cold and lonely Christmas day.*

A Prayer to Serve.

In the Medieval period a rule for nuns was stated in the following prayer:

> *Almighty God, Father, Son and Spirit, who are power, wisdom and love, inspire in me these same three things: power to serve thee, wisdom to please thee and love to do it; power that I may do, wisdom that I may know what to do, love that I may be moved to do all that is pleasing to thee.*

Reward for Service.

Over a pastor's study desk is the following framed prayer by Ignatius Loyola:

> *Teach us, good Lord, to serve you as you deserve; to give and not count the cost, to fight and not to heed the wounds; to toil*

*and not to seek for rest; to labor and not ask for any reward
save that of knowing that we do your will.*

Everyone is Important.

Xvxn though my typxwritxr is an old modxl, it works wxll xxcept
for onx of thx kxys. I'vx wishxd many timxs that it workxd pxrfxctly.
Trux, thxrx arx forty-two kxys that function, but onx kxy not working makxs thx diffxrxncx. Scmxtimxs, it sxxms to mx that our organization is somxwhat likx my typxwritxr — not all thx pxoplx arx
working propxrly. You might say, "Wxll, I'm only onx pxrson. It
won't makx much diffxrxncx." But you sxx, an organization, to bx
xfficixnt, nxxds thx xfforts of xvxry pxrson. Thx nxxt time you think
your xfforts arxn't nxxdxd, rxmxmbxr my typxwritxr, and say to
yourself, "I'm a kxy pxrson and thxy nxxd mx vxry muxh."
(Anonymous)

43

Show and Tell Not!

Jesus Heals a Leper

Mark 1:40-45

(Matthew 8:1-4; Luke 5:12-16)

Epiphany 6

A leper came to him beseeching him, and kneeling said to him, "If you will, you can make me clean." ⁴¹Moved with pity, he stretched out his hand and touched him, and said to him, "I will; be clean." ⁴²And immediately the leprosy left him, and he was made clean. ⁴³And he sternly charged him, and sent him away at once, ⁴⁴and said to him, "See that you say nothing to any one; but go, show yourself to the priest, and offer for your cleansing what Moses commanded, for a proof to the people." ⁴⁵But he went out and began to talk freely about it, and to spread the news, so that Jesus could no longer openly enter a town, but was out in the country; and people came to him from every quarter.

From Bible times until the modern era leprosy has been looked upon with contempt and horror. According to Leviticus 13, the law made a leper wear torn clothes, let his hair hang loose, cry "Unclean!" to anyone approaching and dwell alone outside the camp. In the Middle Ages lepers were not allowed in public buildings or to speak to children. Lepers rang bells to warn others of their presence. In summary, the leper was a despised outcast of society.

Today leprosy is known as Hansen's disease, named for the man who discovered the cause of leprosy. Although ninety-five percent of the world's population seems to be immune from leprosy, there are at least eleven million cases in the world, according to a recent report of the Atlanta Center for Disease Control. In the United States, there are approximately 4,200 cases.

For us to understand and appreciate what leprosy meant to people in Biblical times, we may compare it to AIDS. What leprosy was to people in Jesus' day, AIDS is to us today. Like leprosy was, AIDS is incurable. Both are terminal diseases. An AIDS victim has only a three-year life expectancy. At present it is epidemic. Former Surgeon General C. Everett Kopp reported that AIDS will claim 100 million lives by the year 2000. It is costing Americans two billion dollars annually for research and education related to AIDS. Like leprosy, AIDS sufferers are isolated and discriminated against. AIDS-carrying children are not wanted in schools, and many adults are dismissed from their jobs. Some dentists, physicians and nurses find it difficult and risky to minister to AIDS patients. In some cases, we even reject family members dying of AIDS. Unlike leprosy, AIDS is highly contagious through sexual contact, blood transfusions and polluted needles of drug users. The tragedy is the number of innocent victims of AIDS. By 1988 approximately 500 babies in the United States were born with AIDS and 700 innocent people had contracted the disease through blood transfusions. Leprosy was the curse in Jesus' day, AIDS is the curse for modern times.

As preachers, contronted with today's miracle, are we then in a dilemma? Leprosy is not a problem for most Americans today. And AIDS was non-existent in Jesus' day. If Jesus were alive today, would he be able and willing to touch an AIDS patient and heal him or her of the incurable disease? Mainline church people may believe they are not likely to contract AIDS because they are not for the most part homosexuals and do not indulge in intravenous drug use and leprosy is no longer a probability. So what can this miracle say to us today?

It has been estimated that by the year 1992, every person in American will know at least one person dead or dying from AIDS. AIDS is no longer a "special interest" disease. And even if we are not concerned about contracting leprosy or AIDS, Americans do have a health problem and are in need of physical healing. In 1987 Americans spent a half trillion dollars on health care. We may not be sick in the same way the leper was, but we have our health needs, too. Thus we look to this miracle for help and guidance.

Acclimation

The Gospel Lesson (Mark 1:40-45).
   1. This is the third and last miracle of healing in Mark's first chapter.
   2. The entire Gospel Lesson consists of healing a leper.

3. The Scene: After healing Peter's mother-in-law and others, Jesus leaves Capernaum to preach and heal in other towns. In one of these villages Jesus heals a leper. A few days later he returns to Capernaum. (2:1)

4. Content of the Gospel Lesson —

a. The situation: kneeling a leper begs Jesus to heal him. He has the faith that Jesus is able to heal him of the incurable disease if he would be willing to do so — v. 40

b. Jesus' reaction: compassion and healing — vv. 41-42

c. Jesus' order: show yourself to the priest and tell no one — vv. 43-44

d. The leper's disobedience resulting in a problem for Jesus — v. 45

The Parallels: (Matthew 8:1-4; Luke 5:12-16).

1. The Differences in the Three Accounts:

a. Luke: the leper "fell on his face"; the other two say he knelt.

b. Luke: the leper was "full of leprosy"; calls attention to the seriousness of the disease.

c. Matthew and Luke: the leper calls Jesus "Lord"; The Good News Bible and the Jerusalem Bible translate it "Sir."

d. Matthew: the command to say nothing about the healing is not reported as having been disobeyed.

e. Luke: After the miracle, Jesus withdrew to a lonely place to pray.

2. The Agreement:

a. All three agree that he was a leper.

b. The leper was humble and desperate for help — he knelt or fell on his face.

c. The leper had faith in Jesus' ability to cure the disease.

d. Jesus healed the leper and sent him to report to the priest.

The Lectionary.

Lesson 1 (2 Kings 5:1-14). A top general of the Syrian army, Naaman, contracted leprosy. Upon an Israelite slave-girl's witness that a prophet in Israel could cure him, Naaman goes to Elisha in Israel. When he humbles himself to obey Elisha's order to dip himself seven times in the Jordan River, he is cured.

Relation to the miracle in today's Gospel Lesson:

a. In both Lesson 1 and the Gospel, a man has incurable leprosy.

b. Naaman learns to humble himself like the leper in the miracle.

c. The cure in both cases is simple: for Naaman seven dips in the Jordan; for the leper, only the words of Jesus — "Be clean."

Lesson 2 (1 Corinthians 9:24-27). Like an athlete, Paul disciplines his body by self-control, lest he be disqualified as a preacher of the Gospel. Whereas a winning athlete receives a perishable crown, a Christian receives an imperishable one.

Relation to the Gospel miracle: Lesson 2 deals with the human body and the necessity to keep it under control. The miracle also deals with the human body in need of health.

Gospel (Mark 1:40-45). Jesus left Capernaum to preach in other towns. In one of them a leper approaches him. On his knees he begs Jesus to heal him saying, "You can make me clean if you want to." In response, Jesus says, "I will; be clean." At once the leper was healed. Then Jesus ordered the man to tell no one about the miracle, but to report to the priest for inspection and to get a clean bill of health allowing him to associate with people and to return to his family. Instead, the healed man told everyone what Jesus had done for him. As a result of the publicity, Jesus had to stay in the country where the people came to him for teaching and healing.

Explanation

Leper (v. 40).

In Jesus' day leprosy was the worst thing that could happen to a person. It was a living death. Physically it was a terrifying disease as parts of the body became rotten and fell off. A leper was physically isolated to prevent the disease's spread. The victim was separated from family and community. The person was considered dead, and a funeral service was held for the leper. The diseased one was required by Mosaic Law to live outside the camp and to keep a six-foot distance from every other person. The victim was required to wear torn clothes, to let their hair grow and hang loose and to cry a warning, "Unclean." (Leviticus 13:45)

Kneeling (v. 40).

The leper in the miracle came to Jesus and knelt. The word for "kneel" can also be translated as "worship." Kneeling in this case expresses more than humility or unworthiness. It should be related to the word, "beseeching." (v. 40) This man was desperate for help. He got down on his knees or as Luke reports, he "fell on his face." In Victorian times a woman was begged by a man on his knees to marry him. The leper was so urgent in his plea for a cure that he approached Jesus, law or no law, for the law required him to stay six feet away from a healthy person. It was a case of civil disobedience justified by his terrible need of health. So the leper asked Jesus if he would be willing to heal a law-breaker.

Clean (v. 40).

To be healed was to be made clean. Among the Jews, sin and sickness were related. An unclean person was a sinful one. Leprosy was considered a sign of sin and evil. A leper was required to yell, "Unclean, Unclean!" Today we continue to think of sin as unclean: dirty stories, polluted values, cesspool of iniquity, filthy minds, dirty tricks, etc. When a person commits a crime, we often say, "That person is sick." To be forgiven is to be cleansed. We sing, "Foul, I to the fountain fly; wash me, Savior, or I die." When people commit wrongs, we usually urge them to confess by saying, "Come clean."

Pity (v. 41).

The word, "pity," is sometimes translated as "anger." It is conceivable that Jesus could be angry when he saw what injustice and cruelty was done to lepers. "Pity" is more characteristic of Jesus. He was a man of compassion. His pity was in contrast to the people's attitude toward lepers. They were usually taken for granted and nothing was done to help them. If lepers did not keep their distance, people stoned them to death. People were frightened of lepers because they feared that they themselves might contract the disease. The plight of the leper and his urgent cry for help caused Jesus to pity him.

Touched (v. 41).

Jesus did not have to touch the leper to heal him. He did not have to break the Mosaic Law that a leper was not to be touched.

In other cases, Jesus healed with only a word. The leper had not been touched, not even by wife and children, since he had been declared a leper. That touch was a great and significant act. It brought healing to the doomed man. Moreover, it expressed Jesus' compassion and his acceptance of the leper as he was. Jesus takes us as we are even if diseased and destined for death.

Nothing (v. 44).

When Jesus commanded the leper to say nothing about the healing, he really meant it. Thus, it is said that he "sternly" charged the man to keep the secret. It was not that Jesus was angry as may be implied in the word, "sternly." He felt it was very important that the news should not be spread. Why didn't Jesus want the miracle to be known? Was it a messianic secret to be revealed only at the Cross? To heal a leper was to reveal that the Messiah had come. Jesus did not want the truth to be known at this time because it was not the right time. His messiahship was not to be imposed from without, but it was to be a conclusion from within as the centurion at the Cross confessed, "Truly this man was a Son of God." Moreover, the news of the miracle would cause thousands of lepers to flock to him for healing. Jesus did not want to be confined to being a wonder-worker. He was primarily interested in the spiritual side of humanity, getting us into the Kingdom through repentance and faith. Healing a body or mind may relieve pain and extend life, but death was inevitable. Jesus is primarily concerned about the quality of life resulting from reconciliation with God. To accomplish this he endured the Cross. It was better for people to conclude that he was the Messiah on the basis of what they saw and heard from him. Only then would they be convinced that he was the Christ.

Priest (v. 44).

The leper was ordered to report to the priest for examination and certification that he was cured. This was done in obedience to the Mosaic Law. (Leviticus 14:2-4) The cured leper was to go to the priest. Two birds were sacrificed. One was killed over running water. The other was dipped in the blood of the killed bird and the leper was sprinkled seven times with the bird's blood. Then the leper was declared clean and the remaining bird was allowed to fly away. This order from Jesus showed the religious leaders that he came not to destroy, but to fulfill, the Law. He was not a law-breaker except when the law contradicted the welfare of "man."

49

Application

The Relevance of Revelation.
1. On the surface it may appear that there is little or no relevance of the healing of the leper to our present society. AIDS is our modern leprosy, but there is at present no cure for it, and Jesus is not now on earth to heal it. Nevertheless, the miracle is relevant because it reveals the healing love of Jesus. We suffer from a spiritual leprosy, a sickness unto death which only Christ can cure by his atonement.

2. Where is the Gospel in this miracle? Does the miracle have a good word for people in our time who do not have leprosy or AIDS? The Gospel can be seen in Jesus' ability to heal us. Moreover, he is willing to use that ability to cure the worst malady, and to cure the least worthy to receive it. There is good news in the fact that Jesus, the very Son of God, has a heart of compassion for the afflicted. We see the Gospel in his touch of healing love. If he would make a rotting leper whole, he will be merciful to me in my need.

Sermon Suggestions.
1. Spiritual Leprosy. Sin is the leprosy of the soul. Even more than our bodies, we need a soul cleansing. Like leprosy, sin isolates and segregates us from God and people. Sin is incurable and dooms us to eternal death, which is separation from God. The cure is in Christ who died for our forgiveness. His touch is the beginning of life.

2. An Unbeatable Combination. "If you will, you can make me clean." (v. 40) "Able and willing" constitute an unbeatable combination for success. The problem is when we are able, but not willing, or we are willing and not able to help. In this miracle, Jesus is both willing and able. He is able because as the Son of God, nothing is too hard for him, not even an incurable disease. He is also willing to heal because he not only has the power of God, but also the heart of God, a heart of love and pity. To be a follower of Christ, we need to be both able and willing. We are able because "I can do all things through Christ who strengthens me." We are willing because "The love of Christ compels us."

3. A Possible Impossibility. Suppose Jesus had said to the leper, "I will not," rather than "I will." (v. 41) Jesus would have had every right to say "I will not." This man was breaking the Mosaic Law by coming within the forbidden six-foot distance. Moreover, he could have said, "I will not heal you" because to touch a leper spreads the disease. After all, one must consider self-preservation. Again, why help this leper? He is only one of thousands. He is really a nobody. But for Jesus to have said, "I will not" is a possible impossibility because of his nature, a nature of love. Love makes it impossible for him to say it, or for us to say it.

4. *Righteous Disobedience.* The healing miracle was made possible by disobedience to the Mosaic Law by both parties. On the leper's part, he disobeyed the Law by coming close to Jesus. He was justified in doing so because of his desperate and hopeless condition. Later, he again was disobedient by telling about his healing. Again, he was justified because his joy and gratitude were so powerful that they had to be expressed. On Jesus' part, he, too, broke the Mosaic Law by touching the leper. Love and concern for the leper made him break the Law. The Law is secondary to human welfare. The Law was made for man, not man for the Law. This corresponds to the statement of the Apostles: "We must obey God rather than man."

5. *Keeping a Secret.* Some secrets cannot be kept even if Jesus ordered us to keep them. Jesus sternly commanded the leper not to tell a soul how he was made well. No sooner did he report to the priest, than he told everyone how Jesus healed him. His heart was overflowing with joy and gratitude. He had to tell the good news or burst. It was like telling the tide not to come in or the stars not to shine. Witnessing to what Jesus had done for us is an inner necessity. Evangelism is neither a duty nor a program, but the outpouring of a religious experience with Christ. Our lack of witnessing indicates the absence of a heart-warming experience of Jesus' cleansing from sin.

6. *What the Law Cannot Do.* The Mosaic Law could perhaps retard the spread of leprosy, but it could not cure it. The Law could not keep the leper from coming to Jesus, and the Law could not prevent Jesus from touching the leper. What the Law cannot do, Jesus can. Obedience to the Law through works of righteousness cannot cure sin. Law can neither heal nor save. It takes a Messiah to make things right for us with God. "Thou must save, and thou alone."

Sermon Structures.

1. The Craze to be Clean (v. 40). Many have a craze for cleanliness. We constantly chase dirt. We detest dirt in every form. Each day is wash day. We wash clothes. We shampoo hair, vacuum floors, fill the dishwasher, shower daily and spend millions on soaps and detergents. The leper also had a craze for physical cleanliness to be free from the dirt of leprosy. Like Isaiah, a sinner is one with unclean lips. With the dirt of sin, we cannot come into God's presence. "Who shall ascend unto the hill of the Lord? He that hath clean hands and a pure heart." To be spiritually cleansed:

A. Realize the need for cleansing — "A leper came" (v. 40)
B. Desire to be cleansed — "beseeching him" (v. 40)
C. Believe that Christ can cleanse — "You can" (v. 40)

2. How to Get Cleansed Up (2 Kings 5:1-14; Mark 1:40-45). When we feel dirty or we come in from the garden or work, we often say, "I've got to get cleaned up." A sinner is one who needs spiritual cleansing. The leper was desperate to be clean in health. How can we get spiritually cleaned up?

A. Water of Baptism — Naaman (2 Kings 5:1-14)
B. Blood of Jesus — Holy Communion (Mark 1:40-45)

3. It Takes Two to Succeed (vv. 40-41). It takes two to tango, two to play tennis, two to produce a child. Also, it takes two factors to make success: willingness and ability. Because of both, a leper was healed. We face several possibilities:

A. Willing but not able — "I feel for you but I can't reach you"
B. Able but not willing — hostage takers can free hostages but won't
C. Willing and able — the Jesus way to perform miracles

4. Oh, He Touched Me! (v. 41). Through physical contact, power, blessing and healing may be received. In this sermon we look at several touches —

A. The touch of life — Luke 7:14
B. The touch of pardon — Isaiah 6:7
C. The touch of freedom — Mark 7:33
D. The touch of healing — Mark 1:41

5. Show and Tell Not! (vv. 40-45). The leper was healed. In obedience to the Mosaic Law, the leper was directed to a priest. Jesus ordered the man not to tell a soul how or who healed him. The leper could not keep the secret.

A. Why Jesus did not want it told — find out for yourself
B. Why the leper had to tell — gratitude

6. He is Willing — Are You? (vv. 40-45). The good news of this miracle is that Jesus is willing to help us:

A. Regardless of our condition — "a leper" (v. 40)

B. Regardless of who we are — "If you will" (v. 40)

C. Regardless of opposition to help — "What Moses commanded" (v. 44)

7. How to Get a Miracle (vv. 40-45). Like the leper who won a miracle for himself, anyone today can have a miracle performed in and for a person. The miracle can happen to you if the following conditions are met:

A. Beg — "beseeching him"

B. Believe — "You can make me clean"

C. Obey — "Go, show yourself"

Illustration

Desire for Healing.

Ben, a seven-year-old boy with hemophilia, contracted AIDS from a blood transfusion. The doctors gave Ben one year to live. His parents were unwilling to accept this verdict. Grant, his father, asked, "What do they know of our family? What do they know of our faith?" He was firm in his belief that God would make Ben well. To his wife, Chris, he said, "Miracles do happen, Chris. All we need is time, time for the researchers to find a cure."

Spiritual Cleansing.

The Dome of the Rock in Jerusalem is a very sacred spot for Moslems. This rock is supposed to be on the top of Mt. Moriah, where Abraham was called upon to sacrifice Isaac and where Mohammed left to ascend to heaven. At the foot of the entrance to the magnificent temple there is a circular fountain. Around its base is a ring of stone chairs with a spigot in front of each. Worshipers are required to wash their feet in preparation for going into the mosque. Before entering the temple, everyone is required to take off their shoes because it is considered holy ground. A spiritual cleansing is necessary in order to appear before a holy God.

Touch of Life.

In the Sistine Chapel at the Vatican there is Michelangelo's famous mural of creation. God is shown stretching his arm toward Adam and touching his finger and thus giving him life.

Fellow Lepers.

Father Damien went to the island of Molokai in the Hawaiian Islands to minister to the lepers. After some years he, too, contracted the disease. One Sunday, in his sermon, he revealed that he was a leper, too. He began his sermon, "My fellow lepers, Christ has died for *us*."

Kissing a Leper.

St. Francis of Assisi had a mountain-top religious experience during which he received the stigmata. When he came down the mountain, a leper appeared. He stopped his donkey and climbed down. Slowly he went over to the leper and embraced him. Francis took the leper's face between his hands and kissed his lips. According to legend, the leper was healed by the kiss and his flesh became clean. The kiss of love is a healing agent.

Love for the Afflicted.

In a certain department store a teddy bear sat high on a shelf. Although it had lovely proportions, the brown teddy bear had a problem. Dressed in flashy bib overalls, the button that held one shoulder strap was missing. It drooped by his side; the bib hung in a roll over his chest. Sales persons were too busy to remove the toy. So the little fellow sat accumulating dust. Shopping by herself a little girl came into the toy department and spotted the teddy bear needing attention. She asked to see it, but a clerk tried to dissuade her. She persisted and finally bought it. As she clutched the bear, she was heard saying, "I love you, but you will feel better if I dust you off and sew a button on you."

"He Touched Me."

> Shackled by a heavy burden,
> 'Neath a load of guilt and shame —
> Then the hand of Jesus touched me,
> And now I am no longer the same.
>
> He touched me, Oh he touched me,
> And, Oh, the joy that floods my soul;
> Something happened, and now I know,
> He touched me and made me whole.
> — William J. Gaither

"The Touch of the Master's Hand."

Twas battered and scarred, and the auctioneer
   Thought it scarcely worth his while
To waste much time on the old violin,
   But he held it up with a smile.
"What am I bidden, good folk?" he cried,
   "Who'll start the bidding for me?"
"A dollar — a dollar — then two, only two —
   "Two dollars, and who will make it three?
"Going for three" — but no —
   From the room far back, a gray-haired man
Came forward and picked up the bow.
   Then, wiping the dust from the old violin,
And tightening the loosened strings,
   He played a melody pure and sweet
   As a caroling angel sings.

The music ceased, and the auctioneer,
   With a voice that was quiet and low,
   Said, "Now what am I bid for the old violin?"
   And he held it up with the bow.
"A thousand dollars — and who will make it two?
   "Two thousand — and who'll make it three?
"Three thousand once — three thousand twice —
   "And going — and gone," cried he.
The people cheered, but some of them cried,
   "We do not understand.
"What changed its worth?" Quick came the reply,
   "The touch of the Master's hand."
                 — Myra Brooks Welch

Two-In-One Miracle
The Healing of a Forgiven Paralytic

Mark 2:1-12
(Matthew 9:1-8;
Luke 5:17-26)

Epiphany 7

When he returned to Capernaum after some days, it was reported that he was at home. ²And many were gathered together, so that there was no longer room for them, not even about the door; and he was preaching the word to them. ³And they came, bringing to him a paralytic carried by four men. ⁴And when they could not get near him because of the crowd, they removed the roof above him; and when they had made an opening, they let down the pallet on which the paralytic lay. ⁵And when Jesus saw their faith, he said to the paralytic, "My son, your sins are forgiven." ⁶Now some of the scribes were sitting there, questioning in their hearts, ⁷"Why does this man speak thus? It is blasphemy! Who can forgive sins but God alone?" ⁸And immediately Jesus, perceiving in his spirit that they thus questioned within themselves, said to them, "Why do you question thus in your hearts? ⁹Which is easier, to say to the paralytic, 'Your sins are forgiven,' or to say, 'Rise, take up your pallet and walk'? ¹⁰But that you may know that the Son of man has authority on earth to forgive sins" — he said to the paralytic — ¹¹"I say to you, rise, take up your pallet and go home." ¹²And he rose, and immediately took up the pallet and went out before them all; so that they were all amazed and glorified God, saying, "We never saw anything like this!"

When you get sick, should you call a pastor or a physician, or both? In the case of the paralytic, Jesus indicated that the man needed a pastor rather than a physician. When the paralytic was lowered through the roof of Peter's house, Jesus said, "Your sins are forgiven." Why talk about sins when there appears to be an urgent need for physical healing? Is there a connection between sin and sickness?

A recent study by the National Institute of Allergy and Infectious Diseases was made of the exhausting weakness of the chronic fatigue syndrome. Victims have long bouts of debilitating fatigue as well as fever, sore throat, muscle weakness, and headaches.

The study revealed that the disease eases as the moods of patients improve. Their research strengthened the belief that people's feelings often play a part in their symptoms.

An elderly woman in a New York City hospital continued to get worse when her condition should have been improving. Family therapists discovered that the woman's condition became worse because her two sons fought over who would take the woman home. In the same hospital a Jew regretted the fact that many Jews were killed in the holocaust, and he felt guilty for having been spared. Therapists learned that for years he said prayers of atonement, but when his health prevented him from going to his synagogue, he stopped saying his prayers and his guilt overwhelmed him. His advisors suggested that every day he should do a good deed for someone and tell no one about it. Soon thereafter he was released from the hospital.

Apparently, there is often a connection between sin and sickness. Psychosomatic or holistic medicine recognizes the interdependence and inter-relationships of mind, spirit and body. Accordingly, the whole person is treated by a physician, psychiatrist and pastor. In the case of the paralytic, Jesus saw at once that the man had a spiritual as well as a physical need. Was this man paralyzed, up-tight, and hypertense because of unconfessed sin? If sin were the cause, the cure is forgiveness, which Jesus offered. This pronouncement of mercy infuriated the scribes who considered it blasphemy. By healing the man physically, Jesus demonstrated his authority to forgive sins as well as to heal.

Acclimation

The Gospel Lesson: (Mark 2:1-12).
Jesus left Peter's home in Capernaum to teach and heal in the villages of Galilee, where he healed a leper. Now he comes back to Peter's home, which is so packed with people listening to his preaching that four men carrying a paralytic can not enter through the front door. In desperation they go up the outside stairs to the roof of the one-story house and tear open the roof to let the man come into Jesus' immediate presence. Jesus interrupts his sermon to say, "Your sins are forgiven." This shocks the scribes, who think, "This is blasphemy, for only God can forgive sin." Reading their minds,

Jesus asks them which is easier — to heal or to forgive. To prove that he has the authority to forgive, he tells the paralytic to get up, take up his bed, and go home. Immediately the man obeys and the people are astonished.

The miracle is the first of five that deal with the opposition of the religious leaders to Jesus' ministry. (Mark 2:1—3:7) In this case, they object to his claim to forgive sin. They consider it blasphemy when a human claims to do what only God can do.

New Testament scholars are divided on the question of whether this pericope is an account of a composite miracle. Does this miracle consist of one or two accounts? Some hold that the miracle consists of two strands of tradition. The earlier account eliminates verses 6 to 10. If these verses are omitted, the miracle is a statement of forgiveness and healing which occur simultaneously because the Jews believed that a cure was dependent upon forgiveness. For them, sickness was the result of sin. The other strand, verses 6 to 10, is the product of the church which wanted to explain and justify the practice of forgiving sin in the name of Christ. If the two strands are put together as in the present pericope, forgiveness and healing are separate. The healing came after Jesus' response to the scribes. If saying, "Your sins are forgiven" is easier, in the public's mind, than to heal, Jesus proves by doing the more difficult that he has the authority to forgive sins.

The Parallels: (Matthew 9:1-8; Luke 5:17-26)

1. Differences in the accounts:

Matthew — omits the tearing up of the roof to let down the paralytic to Jesus.

Mark — only Mark mentions that four men did the carrying.

Luke — Not only the scribes but also the Pharisees from all over Galilee, Judea, and Jerusalem came to hear Jesus teach. Also, Luke describes a Roman house by the removal of tiles from the roof. Mark has a Palestinian house in mind involving a roof of brushwood and mud.

2. Agreements:

The three accounts agree:
— Jesus forgave the paralytic's sins
— The faith of others prompted the miracle
— The scribes charged Jesus with blasphemy
— The paralytic was healed
— People glorified God for the miracle

58

The Lectionary: (Epiphany 7).

Lesson 1: (Isaiah 43:18-25). God's people are held in bondage by the Babylonians. Through the prophet, Yahweh tells the exiles not to think only of past deliverance from Egypt, but to think of what he *will* do. Yahweh will free the Jews from the Babylonians. They are in this bondage because they neglected worship and became tired of God. Likewise, Yahweh became tired of their sins. However, he forgives and forgets their sin.

The relation to the Gospel's miracle is: As Yahweh is a God of forgiveness, his Son forgives sin and heals the consequences of sin.

Lesson 2: (2 Corinthians 1:18-22) The Corinthian congregation is upset with Paul for not coming to Corinth as he had promised. He had a change in travel plans and did not visit the church. It appeared as though he were fickle and did not keep his promises. Paul assured the congregation that Jesus is not Yes and No, but always Yes. Christ fulfills all promises. His promise to Christians is guaranteed by the gift of the spirit.

The relation to the Gospel's miracle: Jesus keeps his promise to forgive our sins. We can count on that promise which results in our becoming his children. The presence of the Holy Spirit in our lives is proof that his promise of forgiveness has been fulfilled.

Gospel: (Mark 2:1-12). Jesus' teaching in Peter's home at Capernaum is interrupted when four men lower a paralyzed man on a pallet. Immediately, Jesus sees that the man needs spiritual healing. Thus, he assures the man that his sins are forgiven. This arouses the ire of the religious leaders who charge Jesus with blasphemy. They claim that only God can forgive sins. In response, Jesus asks them whether it is easier to say, "Your sins are forgiven" or "Get up and walk." To show that it is easier to say, "Your sins are forgiven," he orders the paralytic to get up, take up his bed, and go home. When the people see him do this, they are amazed and exclaim, "We never saw anything like this before."

The relation of this miracle to the Epiphany Season: This is the season when the glory of God is manifested in Christ. In today's miracle, the authority of Jesus to forgive sins is seen. Since only God can forgive sin, we see in Jesus the only Son of God, who, by virtue of his authority to forgive, becomes the world's Savior. By forgiving sin he manifests the glory and grace of God.

Explanation

At home (v. 1).

Jesus was "at home." Whose home in Capernaum? Probably it was Peter's home in which a short time ago he had healed Peter's mother-in-law. At that time a Palestinian home usually had one room and a flat roof. A stairway on the outside of the house led to the roof. The roof was built with wooden beams overlaid with branches and gravel. When an opening was made to lower the paralytic, there probably was a lot of dirt and dust that came down on the people assembled in the house.

Word (v. 2).

The house was jammed with people eager to hear Jesus. There was not even standing room, and the roof had to be torn up to get the man to Jesus. According to the account, Jesus was not at the time healing or performing miracles that would draw a crowd. He was preaching the "Word." What was his message? What could be so attractive, interesting, and dynamic that it drew a crowd? The "word" was the Good News: the Kingdom of God was near; repent and believe the Gospel. (Mark 1:15) This is still the secret of packing a church — dynamic preaching of the Word. People will go where they are fed and helped.

Paralytic (v. 3).

The paralytic is one of the least known characters in the miracles. We know practically nothing about him, except that he was paralyzed. We do not know his name, his family, his home or his work. We do not know what caused his paralysis. Mark does not tell whether he wanted to be healed or whether he believed in Jesus. We are not sure he was grateful for the healing. What were his sins that were forgiven? It seems he was only a passive participant. Four men carried him to Jesus. He was forgiven and healed on the basis of the faith of others. The people glorified God for the healing while the paralytic was on his way home. All was done for him by his friends and Jesus. Not a word came from his lips. The most he did was to get up, pick up his bed, and go home. It is a picture of pure and simple grace.

Their faith (v. 5).

The four men had faith that Jesus could make the paralytic walk again. If they did not believe it, they would not have burdened themselves by carrying him to where Jesus was preaching. Their faith was proved by their determination to get the man to Jesus regardless of what it took. It meant tearing up a man's roof and then having the expense of repairing it. On the basis of their faith, the paralytic was forgiven and healed. It was a case of vicarious faith.

Sins (v. 5).

What is the relation of sin and sickness? Are they connected? Is every sickness the result of sin? In the Old Testament all suffering is believed to result from sin, separation from God. Was this not the issue in the case of Job? Every disease, including death, was considered the work of demons. To be healed, then, is to first be forgiven. Sickness can result from sin. Holistic medicine recognizes this. But, not all sickness or tragedy can be sin-caused. Jesus pointed this out in Luke 13:2-5 and John 9:3. In today's miracle a paralyzed man was a forgiven person. After a controversy with the scribes, the healing took place. If the opposition of the scribes did not occur, forgiveness and healing were simultaneous, showing that the man's sins caused the paralysis. If the opposition took place, forgiveness and healing were independent.

Scribes (v. 6).

The scribes were among the religious leaders of Jesus' time and constituted a powerful organization. The first seats at the synagogue were reserved for them. They had places at the head tables. They wore special clothing in keeping with their position. The scribes were biblical scholars, experts in the Torah. They interpreted the Law for the nation. To protect the Law, they had other precepts that prescribed minute ceremonial observances.

Blasphemy (v. 7).

When Jesus assured the paralytic that his sins were forgiven, the scribes cried, "Blasphemy." They were right by contending that only God can forgive sins. To pose as God, and to try to do what only God can do, is indeed most sacrilegious. Blasphemy was considered reason for execution. The scribes lacked the insight to see in Jesus the "Son of man," the Messiah, God's only Son. They did not realize that this man was also "the word became flesh."

61

Easier (v. 8).

How was Jesus to answer this charge of blasphemy? He answered it by asking the scribes a question, "Which is easier . . . ?" From the human viewpoint it is very easy to say the words, "You are forgiven." Whether or not you are forgiven cannot be demonstrated. But, here is a man lying flat on his back who cannot move a muscle. Who has the power to enable him to stand up, carry his bed and walk home? Or, here is a person of ill repute with terminal cancer. Anyone can say, "Your sins are forgiven," but who can say, "Your cancer is in remission?" So, Jesus uses this logic: if I can heal the paralysis, then I can do the easier thing of forgiving. The truth is that only God has the power and authority to forgive and to heal. Nevertheless, a sick person can be a forgiven sinner.

Perceiving (v. 8).

Jesus had marvelous insight. This is demonstrated in the healing of the paralytic. First, he perceived that the paralytic's problem was spiritual and not physical. Thus, he said upon seeing him, "Your sins are forgiven." Next, he perceived the faith in the hearts of the men who carried the paralytic to him and who tore open the roof. Third, he perceived what the scribes were thinking about his forgiving as blasphemy. They did not say a word, but he heard their thoughts. Jesus knows what is in human beings — what they are thinking, planning and dreaming. There is no hiding place from Christ!

Application

Relevance of Revelation.

1. This miracle of healing the paralytic touches our lives in the area of health. When one gets sick, is it a pastor or a physician who is really needed? This is related to psychosomatic symptoms and holistic medicine. It is common knowledge that guilt, anxiety, fear and stress can cause physical problems such as ulcers, skin diseases, hypertension, heart attacks, etc. This leads to the question of the relationship between sickness and sin.

2. The miracle is related to our lives in the universal human need of forgiveness. Is there a modern need for forgiveness? That depends upon our consciousness of sin. What then is sin? Further, who is able to forgive? Where does one go for divine forgiveness today? In a day when retaliation and revenge are the accepted response to evil doings, how can we persuade people to forgive their enemies?

3. The identity of Jesus is involved in this miracle. If Jesus is only a human, he, as the scribes said, is guilty of blasphemy. If he is God in the flesh, he has the authority to forgive sins. It is surprising that Jesus refers to himself as the Messiah in the term, "Son of man," since heretofore he has wanted this to be a messianic secret. In our day, is there a problem in getting people to recognize his deity?

4. Basic truths for our time:
— forgiveness can cure illness
— the authority of Jesus to forgive sins
— the faith that leads to healing
— the efficacy of vicarious faith

Sermon Suggestions:

1. Giving Jesus a Home. Mark says that when Jesus returned to Capernaum, he was "at home." This implies that Jesus had a home in Capernaum, but we know that he left his paternal home in Nazareth and that thereafter "the Son of man had no place to lay his head." Since he was in Peter's home earlier and healed Peter's mother-in-law, we assume he was "at home" in Peter's house. Jesus has no home but our homes. When we invite Jesus into our homes, they become his homes, too. He uses our homes to preach and heal. The sermon may ask, "Is your home Jesus' home also?"

2. Get Carried Away. Four men put a paralyzed man on a stretcher and literally carried the man to Jesus. They did not call a taxi to take the sick man. They did not pay someone to take him. They literally carried the needy man. This is an important technique for today's evangelism. An invitation is good; a visit to a prospect's home is better. The best is to come with your car and pick up the prospects and carry them to church. Many were carried by their parents for baptism. Parents chauffeur their children to church school. Shut-ins and the aged are carried to church on a church bus. People need the healing of Christ. They may not come on their own. Is there enough faith and love on our part to carry them to Jesus?

3. Popular Preaching. Peter's home was a packed house, floor-to-floor, with people gathered to hear Jesus preach. There were no miracles to draw a crowd, only a sermon. They came to hear "the word." (v. 2) The "Word" was the Good News that God's Kingdom had come. Jesus called upon the people to repent and believe. In our day, what will pack our churches? In a time when many say, "Don't preach to me," what kind of sermons will draw crowds, crowds like we see at football games? No better answer can be given than what Jesus did — preach the Word. The Gospel feeds, blesses, and challenges. People flock to the churches where they are spiritually fed with the Word.

4. *Vicarious Faith.* Is personal faith a "must" to be healed or blessed? Here is a case of one who expressed no faith. But, Jesus saw the faith of those who brought the paralytic — "saw their faith." (v. 5) An objection to infant baptism is that the child is too young to have faith. Consequently, among some Christians, only adult baptism is administered. However, the vast majority of Christians baptize infants because sponsors have faith for the child. Intercessory prayer also is acceptable because of the faith of those who pray for others.

5. *Who Forgives?* The scribes objected to Jesus' forgiving the paralytic. They were correct in maintaining that only God can forgive sin. How does God forgive sin today? God forgives through human instrumentality. God forgave the paralytic through Jesus. Today God forgives through the church. Jesus gave the church the power of the keys: "If you forgive the sins of any, they are forgiven." (John 20:23) God forgives through individual Christians: "as we forgive those . . ." If we forgive, God the Spirit caused us to forgive. If only God can forgive, it follows that all evil doings are sins not only against humanity but against God.

6. *The Easy Way.* The impression one gets from the question of Jesus, whether it is easier to forgive than to heal, is that forgiveness is easier. If, then, he does the more difficult, he must be able to do the easier. However, forgiveness is harder, because only God can do it. To forgive us, it cost God the death of his beloved Son. For us, forgiveness is most difficult when we truly forgive. To heal a physical disease is difficult, but to heal a relationship with God or a fellow being is far harder. Perhaps that explains why there is so little genuine forgiveness among us.

7. *Call a Pastor!* The paralytic did not need a physical healer. He needed someone to say, "Your sins are forgiven." His physical problem had its source in his spiritual condition. Doctors report that many of their patients are not physically but spiritually sick, resulting in physical ailments. Illnesses can result from guilt, hatred,

fear and anxiety. These indicate that there is a disturbed relationship with God. Get at peace with God, and peace of mind usually results. With peace of mind comes a healthier body.

Sermon Structures

1. What is Your Reaction? (vv. 1-12). Various reactions resulted from the miracle. Which is yours?

A. Faith — the four men — v. 5

B. Anger — the scribes — vv. 6, 7

C. Praise — the people — v. 12

2. The High Cost of Forgiveness (vv. 1-12). Is it really more difficult to heal than to forgive? Count the cost of forgiveness:

A. The cost to God — the Cross

B. The cost to us to be forgiven — repentance — forgiveness of others

C. The cost for us to forgive

— Forgo revenge

— Absorb the hurt

— Accept the forgiven one

3. The Sickness of Sin (vv. 1-12). Sin and sickness can be related as seen in the paralytic. This leads us to consider:

A. Sickness may result from sin

B. One can be healed, but not forgiven

C. One can be forgiven, but not healed

4. Can One Believe for Another? (vv. 1-12). The healing and forgiving of the paralytic teaches us that we can be healed and forgiven on the basis of faith of others. What vicarious faith can do:

A. Faith brings people to Christ — v. 3

B. Faith brings forgiveness — v. 5

C. Faith brings health — v. 10

5. If Only God Can Forgive (vv. 1-12). The scribes were right when they claimed that only God can forgive, because sin is a matter between God and the person. The implications of this truth:

A. All evil thoughts, words and deeds are sins against God

B. Jesus can forgive because he is God's Son

C. God the Spirit authorizes us to forgive

6. Who Can Forgive? (vv. 1-12). Who can say today, "Your sins are forgiven"?

A. God says it in Christ — v. 5

B. God says it through the church — John 20:23

C. God says it through Christians — ". . . As we forgive . . ."

7. What is the Hardest Thing to Do? (vv. 9-11). Often one hears, "It was the hardest thing I ever had to do." If God alone can forgive sin, how can we do what God does? For some the hardest thing to do is to forgive. Why is this so?

A. Forgiveness requires foregoing retaliation

B. Forgiveness demands forgetting the offense

C. Forgiveness calls for forgiving self.

Illustration

What is Forgiveness?

According to Kenneth Chafin:

> *Forgiveness isn't pretending nothing has happened, or pretending that what happened didn't hurt. It isn't even forgetting it completely, and it isn't going back and starting over as though it hadn't ever happened. Instead, forgiveness is refusing to let anything permanently destroy the relationship. There's a place for saying, "I'm sorry." There's a place for assuring the other person that "all is forgiven." But the goal of both is to rebuild the relationship.*

God's Business?

Heinrich Heine: "I love to sin. God loves to forgive sin. Really, this world is admirably arranged."

After listening to a discussion by a group of theologians, a student said, "I almost get the feeling that the Christian has a kind of obligation to sin, so that God gets to do his thing."

No Forgiveness.

In his autobiography, Lee Iacocca declared: "Henry Ford made my kids suffer, and for that I'll never forgive him."

Simon Wiesenthal was a prisoner in a forced labor camp. He was working in a hospital where a young Nazi officer lay wounded and dying. He made Wiesenthal listen while he confessed his atrocities, including burning down a houseful of Jews in the Ukraine and shooting those who tried to escape. The German trooper was tormented by guilt and begged Wiesenthal, as a Jew, to forgive him. Wiesenthal turned and walked away. He survived the camp and spent the next forty years hunting Nazi war criminals.

Sin or Sickness?

A certain man came home drunk. His wife helped him to his room, to undress, and then she knelt by the bed and asked, "John, do you want me to pray for you?" He nodded affirmatively. She prayed, "Dear Lord, I pray for my husband who lies here drunk . . . ." Before she could finish her prayer, he gruffly said, "Don't tell him I'm drunk; tell him I'm sick."

Self Forgiveness.

A mother tells of leaving her husband for another man. She became pregnant by this man. When her new lover learned of the pregnancy, he gave her something to swallow in the hope of inducing an abortion. When that failed, he abandoned her. Eventually, the woman returned to her husband, who forgave her and treated her child as though he were his own son. At age three the child died of cancer. The mother worried whether what she swallowed had caused the cancer. Though her Christian faith preached forgiveness, she could not forgive herself. When she finally did forgive herself, she underlined every passage in her Bible that referred to God's forgiveness and was amazed that her burden was lifted.

Reconciliation through Forgiveness.

There was a feud between Thomas Jefferson and John Adams. They became enemies when Jefferson defeated Adams for a second term as president in 1800. On the eve of his inauguration, Jefferson went to the White House to tell Adams that he hoped the bitter campaign had not damaged their friendship. Before Jefferson could say a word, Adams raved, "You have turned me out! You have turned me out!" For the next eleven years they did not speak to each other. When some of Jefferson's friends visited Adams in Boston, the old man confessed, "I always loved Jefferson and I still love him." Jefferson's neighbors gave this report to Jefferson, urging him to let Adams know of his affection. This began a great correspondence in American history with an exchange of views on politics, philosophy and religion.

A Test Case Miracle

The Case of the	Mark 2:23—3:6
Paralyzed	Mark 3:1-6
Hand	(Matthew 12:9-14; Luke 6:6-11)

Pentecost 2

One sabbath he was going through the grainfields; and as they made their way his disciples began to pluck ears of grain. ²⁴And the Pharisees said to him, "Look, why are they doing what is not lawful on the sabbath?" ²⁵And he said to them, "Have you never read what David did, when he was in need and was hungry, he and those who were with him: ²⁶how he entered the house of God, when Abiathar was high priest, and ate the bread of the Presence, which it is not lawful for any but the priests to eat, and also gave it to those who were with him?" ²⁷And he said to them, "The sabbath was made for man, not man for the sabbath; ²⁸so the Son of man is lord even of the sabbath."

Again he entered the synagogue, and a man was there who had a withered hand. ²And they watched him, to see whether he would heal him on the sabbath, so that they might accuse him. ³And he said to the man who had the withered hand, "Come here." ⁴And he said to them, "Is it lawful to do good or to do harm, to save life or to kill?" But they were silent. ⁵And he looked around at them with anger, grieved at their hardness of heart, and said to the man, "Stretch out your hand." He stretched it out, and his hand was restored. ⁶The Pharisees went out, and immediately held counsel with the Herodians against him, how to destroy him.

The miracle of healing the withered hand is not a usual miracle in which someone comes to Jesus begging for healing. In this case, the man makes no request for help; he is just a worshiper in the congregation. Moreover, the miracle need not have been performed on the sabbath, since the man was not threatened with death. To avoid a conflict with his enemies, Jesus could have healed the hand later that day at sundown, the end of the sabbath day.

But, there was a principle at stake here. Jesus used the miracle as a test case, a case study, an "Exhibit A." Jesus called the man to come to the front so that all could see him with his paralyzed

68

hand. Here he is! What shall be done — a miracle or not on the sabbath day? Jesus raised the question for the congregation to decide: "Is it lawful on the sabbath to do good or to do harm, to save life or to kill?"

It is a question about what can or cannot be done on the sabbath. This is not really a question for us in the 1990s. We have an open Sunday to do anything we want — to work, to play, or to worship. A better question for us, "Is there anything we may not do on Sunday?"

Behind the surface, the question about how to deal with the sabbath (Christian Sunday), is a very important principle that affects us today as much as it did the people in Jesus' day. It is a question about living by the spirit or the letter of the law. Are we to follow the theology of Jesus or of the Pharisees? Which is more important: a law or a human? Are our open Sundays, when anything goes, a threat to religious faith and practice?

These are the questions we are called upon to struggle with as we deal with this miracle in preaching. We will be preaching not so much on the miracle as on a principle rooted in the teachings of Jesus. Once again, Jesus brings the man with the afflicted hand into our midst as a case study for us to come to a decision. The principle applies not only to one day of the week, but to every day.

Acclimation

The Setting.

Mark 2:23—3:6 is the Gospel Lesson for Pentecost 2 in the Common and Roman Catholic lectionaries. The Lutheran lectionary uses only 2:23-28. The probable reason for adding 3:1-16 is the miracle of the paralyzed hand. The miracle fits into the previous discussion Jesus had with the Pharisees concerning his hungry Disciples who on a sabbath day, were picking and eating wheat as they passed through a field.

Later on the same day, Jesus goes to the synagogue in Capernaum where there is a man with a paralyzed hand. Would Jesus again break the sabbath law by healing the man? He asks the man to come forward for the people to see him. As "Exhibit A," he asks the congregation whether it is lawful to do good on the sabbath. To show that he was lord of the sabbath, Jesus healed the withered hand.

69

By adding the miracle to the original pericope, we see that it is not only a good use of the sabbath to get food for the hungry, but to do good of any kind.

The Situation.

Jesus is in a growing conflict with the religious leaders. They were appalled when he forgave the sins of the paralytic. (2:1-12) They were displeased with him for eating with outcasts and tax collectors. (2:15-17) They found fault with the lack of fasting on the part of the disciples. (2:18-22) They accused him of breaking the sabbath law by allowing his hungry disciples to pluck and eat wheat as they passed through a field. Now he heals a man even on the sabbath. This is the straw that breaks the camel's back. His enemies meet to plot his destruction.

The Parallel Passages: (Matthew 12:1-14; Luke 6:1-11)

Differences:

Matthew:

1. The Pharisees open up the subject with the question: "Is it lawful to heal on the sabbath?" — v. 10

2. Only Matthew refers to the sheep fallen into a pit on the sabbath — v. 11

3. Matthew does not have the man with the withered hand come forward

Mark

1. Without asking any questions, Jesus calls the man to the front — v. 3

2. Only Mark notes that there was silence following the question — v. 4

3. Only Mark reports that Jesus expressed anger and grief — v. 5

4. Only Mark says that the Pharisees and Herodians joined to plot Jesus' death — v. 6

Luke

1. Only Luke notes that Jesus perceived what the Pharisees were thinking — v. 8

2. Only Luke reports that at the end of the miracle the Pharisees were furious — v. 11

3. Only Luke tells us that it was the man's right hand that was withered — v. 6

Agreement:

1. Jesus' enemies gathered to find reason to arrest Jesus for breaking the sabbath law.

2. A man with a withered hand was healed by the same words: "Stretch out your hand."

3. The question of Jesus: "Is it lawful to do good on the sabbath?"

4. The reaction was the same: Jesus' enemies plot his death.

The Lectionary: (Pentecost 2).

Lesson 1 (1 Samuel 16:1-3). This is the first of a series of fourteen lessons on the life of David. The series lends itself to a string (probably too long) of biographical sermons. Consequently, the First Lesson is not intentionally related to the other Lessons.

Lesson 2 (2 Corinthians 4:5-12). Likewise, this pericope is the first of a series of six lessons from 2 Corinthians. Again, the series suggests a series of sermons. A series of six is the usual length for a series. Accordingly, the Second Lesson is not necessarily related to the other two Lessons.

Gospel (Mark 2:23—3:6). This Sunday is the starting time for three stories. Today's Gospel is the first of eight taken from the first six chapters of Mark. The Gospels for Series B are, for the most part, taken from Mark. The in-course coverage of Mark is resumed this Sunday (Pentecost 2). The Gospel Lesson for Epiphany 8 was Mark 2:18-22 (Jesus explains why his disciples did not fast). Mark's account of Jesus' ministry is continued with the very next verse, 23 (the first verse of today's Gospel). Except for Christ the King Sunday (the last Sunday of the church year), the Gospels are taken from Mark, chapters 2—13. The long series from Mark is given a welcome break with five Sundays dealing with John 6 (Pentecost 10-14).

Explanation

Man (v. 1).

Who was this man? No name is given. It could be any man with a serious need. The name is not important. He is relatively unimportant, for the spotlight is on Jesus and what he would do about this man's need of healing. Nothing is known of this man, but such knowledge is not necessary. The issue is whether a good deed should be done on a sabbath day.

Hand (v. 1).

Trouble with a hand does not appear to be a crisis. It is not like blindness or leprosy. Luke tells us that it was his right hand. This detail indicates that the hand was vital to the man's well-being. According to tradition, he was a mason. Without the use of his right hand, he could not work at his skill. Without work, he could not provide for his family. It meant that he had to beg for food. The Gospel according to the Hebrews says, "I was a mason, seeking a living with my hands; I beg you, Jesus, to restore my health to me, so that I need not beg for my food in shame."

Accuse (v. 2).

Jesus did not have a sympathetic audience. His enemies watched to see if he would break the Mosaic Law by working (healing) on the sabbath. They watched, not as interested spectators, but as enemies with murder in their hearts. They were out to get him, but they needed a specific case. Ironically, his enemies were religious leaders: Pharisees, scribes, Herodians.

Sabbath (vv. 2, 4).

Sabbath is a Hebrew word meaning "rest." It was the seventh day of the week, in observance of God's work of creation for six days and of his rest on the seventh. Since the fourth century, the Christian sabbath has been observed on the first day of the week in celebration of the Resurrection. It is now known as "the Lord's Day." Jews continue to observe the seventh day (Saturday) as the day of rest, and certain Christian groups also observe the sabbath on Saturday.

The observance of the sabbath was the hallmark of Judaism. It is rooted in the commandment, "Remember the sabbath day to keep it holy." To prevent the breaking of this law, the Jews added a great mass of related rules. Every faithful Jew strictly observed the sabbath as a mark of their piety. A Jew would even give up his life to obey it. In the light of the law's extreme importance, one can understand why the religious leaders were upset with Jesus' seeming disregard of the law. Jesus' principle was that human life was more important and sacred than the sabbath law. Therefore, to do good and to heal a person on the sabbath was no violation of the law. For the Jewish leaders, the Law came first and human welfare came second. That was the issue brought to a head at the time of this miracle.

Silent (v. 4).

Jesus asked his opponents whether on the sabbath it was lawful to do good or to do harm. They were silent. They were convinced that the sabbath was not a day to do either good or harm. They were positive they were right. Their purpose in observing Jesus was not to argue, but to get evidence of his breaking the Law that they might have him arrested. The Pharisees declined the opportunity to argue, discuss, and debate the question because they already believed they had the anser.

Anger (v. 5).

Jesus looked with anger upon his opponents. Anger is a natural and normal emotion. The lack of anger is a deficiency of the soul. The issue is getting angry for the right reason. Jesus was never angry when he suffered abuse, but became angry when others were oppressed. He was angry when he saw the blasphemous use of the temple. Here he was angry over their short-sightedness and insensitivity to a man's need.

Grieved (v. 5).

At the same time Jesus was angry, he was also grieved at their hardness of heart. He tempered his anger with grief as justice should be tempered with mercy. He felt sorry for these religious leaders — for their lack of compassion and their moral blindness. They were spiritually sick people, and he felt sorry for them. It is a mixture of emotions, a contrast, yet they are very closely associated with each other. Anger without sorrow is dangerous, for it becomes destructive. Sorrow without anger is non-productive.

Stretch (v. 5).

Here is a command to do the impossible. How could a withered, paralyzed, shriveled hand be stretched out? It is like telling a blind person to look! Jesus commanded the man to stretch out his paralyzed hand. With the command came the healing, and the man was able to do it. The man's obedience resulted in the restoration of his hand's health. The hand was completely "restored." It was not merely soothed or massaged, but restored — as good as new.

Herodians (v. 6).

The Herodians who teamed up with Pharisees to destroy Jesus were friends and supporters of King Herod Antipas. They supported

Herod's government and were friends of Rome, which appointed Herod as king. Jesus' popularity and teachings posed a threat to the peace of the status quo. They feared an uprising against the government, and that they in turn would lose their place of privilege and financial well-being. The Pharisees opposed Jesus for religious reasons and the Herodians for political reasons. They could work together because they had a common fear and enemy.

Application

Relevance of Revelation.
   1. Open or Closed Sunday? The miracle in today's Gospel deals with a tightly closed sabbath. The issue in Jesus' day was the possibility of opening the day to do a good work. This is not our problem in today's society. We have an open Sunday, open to anything — to work, to play, to worship — except to crime, a prohibition not limited to Sundays. Then the question was, "Can we do a good deed on the sabbath without breaking the law?" Now the question is, "Since anything can be done on the sabbath, is there anything we can't do?" Or, is there anything we should not do on Sunday?
   2. Is Today's Open Sunday a Threat to Religious Faith and Practice? In today's America, Sunday is almost like any other day of the week. We can shop on Sundays, attend athletic games, and do just about anything you can think of. Has this open Sunday worked to the detriment of the church? Are people more interested in recreation than in religion? Do they prefer to work rather than to worship? Modern society has done away with the Blue Laws prohibiting work and commercial entertainment. Have we gone too far in opening up Sunday?
   3. Sabbath or Sunday? There is still a controversy over the day of the sabbath. For Jews the sabbath is Saturday, the seventh day of the week, a day of rest as God rested the seventh day after Creation. Certain Christian groups, holding to a literal interpretation of the Scriptures, still observe Saturday as the sabbath. In the fourth century, the church decided that Sunday would be the sabbath for Christians, in observance of Jesus' Resurrection on the first day of the week. It initiated the custom to refer to Sunday as "The Lord's Day." For Christians, every day is the Lord's day, a day to serve and glorify God. One day is no better, nor more holy, than another.

74

But, Sunday is different by being a day set aside to worship publicly and to rest.

4. Letter or Spirit? The problem of the proper observance of the sabbath points to a more basic question which still is very much alive today. It is not so much what we do, or do not do, on Sunday as it is our attitude toward the law, "Remember the sabbath day to keep it holy." Do we go by the letter or by the spirit of the law? Which is more important: a law or the welfare of a person? This is the question Jesus raised in the synagogue. If we live by the letter of the law, we may become literalists and fundamentalists. The law becomes a moral straitjacket, and we are prisoners of the law. The letter kills, but the spirit gives life. This question makes the miracle relevant to us today.

Sermon Suggestions.

1. The Law — Good or Bad? For the man with the withered hand, the breaking of the Law would have been good. For the Pharisees the breaking of the Law would have been bad. There is the issue to be faced in the sermon. Can a law be good or bad for people? The Law was meant for our good. Jesus said he did not come to destroy the Law but to fulfill it. If the Law is used as an end in itself, it can be bad for people. Yet, without Law, society would experience chaos.

2. Is Civil Disobedience a Virtue? In this miracle story, the Herodians and Pharisees plotted to end Jesus' civil disobedience of healing on the sabbath. The Herodians wanted no civil protests or riots against the government of Herod lest they lose their favored positions. They were for law and order. Following Jesus' attitude toward the Law, Christians may participate in civil disobedience when a law is a bad law causing injustice and discrimination. It is a question of obeying God rather than man.

3. Law or Love? At the healing of the paralyzed hand, the question was whether Law or love should prevail. The Pharisees had hearts of murder, demanding that the Law must be obeyed at all costs. Jesus had a heart of love for the afflicted man and wanted to help him. For Jesus love was more important than a law. Let the Law go hang! A higher law permits one doing good on the sabbath.

4. Holy Anger. Jesus looked at the Pharisees with anger. It is a natural and normal emotion that every human experiences. It is another piece of evidence that Jesus was fully human. It is not a matter of being angry, but the reason for it. Jesus was never angry for things done to himself. He was angry when he saw the abuse of the temple; when he saw the hatred and lack of compassion on the part of the Pharisees. He was angry that they were that way. But he tempered his anger with grief. At the same time he was sorry they had that attitude.

5. *Who is Jesus?* Who is this man who dares to break the Mosaic Law of the sabbath? This is the Jews' most sacred day, the hallmark of their faith. The sabbath was for spiritual nurture and physical rest. Even after the creation, God rested. Who is this Jesus who goes against God? Is he greater than God? Openly and daringly Jesus allows his Disciples to gather food on the sabbath and defies the religious leaders by healing on the sabbath. Who does he think he is? Who do the people think he is? In verse 28 he claims that he, the Son of man, is lord of the sabbath. He is claiming to be the Messiah, to be God's Son, and therefore lord of the sabbath. If he made the Law in the beginning, he has authority to obey, disobey or change it.

6. *The Danger of Religious Extremists.* There is no class of people more dangerous than fanatical religious people. In the miracle account, the Pharisees, scribes and Herodians were in ''church'' to worship. Yet, they opposed Jesus with murder in their hearts. They were not really in the synagogue to worship, but to get something on Jesus. After the service they met to consider how they could kill Jesus. And these were religious people! They were in church! We saw what atrocities occurred when Moslem fundamentalists took over the government in Iran. Religious fanatics go after their opponents in ''holy'' wars. By dying for their cause, they believe they are promised an immediate paradise. Today, church people can hate each other with acrimony resulting in schisms.

7. *You Decide!* Jesus uses a technique here which he often used at other times. He uses the inductive method of presenting an issue, asking a question, and calling upon the people to decide. The issue is: heal or not on the sabbath? Is it lawful or not? So, he uses a concrete case of a man in the congregation with a withered hand. He calls the man to come up front so all could see him and his hand. With this exhibit, Jesus asks whether it is lawful on the sabbath to do good or to do harm, to save life or to kill. He waits for an answer, but none comes. His answer is not verbal, but in the act of healing the hand. What constitutes acceptable behavior on a Sunday is for each person to decide in light of Jesus' example.

Sermon Structures.

1. What Jesus Can Do for You (3:1-6). What Jesus did for the unknown man in the miracle, Jesus can do for you.

A. Jesus can give you health, healing — v. 5

B. Jesus can provide work, livelihood — healed hand

C. Jesus can restore your self-esteem — no longer a beggar

2. The Case for Civil Disobedience (2:23—3:6). Today people engage in civil disobedience to change laws that cause injustice. By healing a man on the sabbath, Jesus could be accused of civil disobedience. Civil disobedience is justified when:

A. People need food — vv. 23-24

B. People are hurting — 3:1-2

— Denied civil rights

— Suffer discrimination

3. An Impossible Command (3:5b). Have you ever said, "I can't do it. It is impossible. Too much is expected of me"? The man with the paralyzed hand must have felt that way when Jesus ordered him to "Stretch out your hand." How could anyone move a paralyzed, withered hand? See how he did it:

A. The divine command — "Stretch"

B. Obedience — "He stretched it"

C. Restoration — "His hand was restored"

4. Do You Have a Right to be Angry? (3:5a). Anger is a normal emotion, but it needs to be used rightly. Jesus was angry with the Pharisees for objecting to the healing of a man on the sabbath. When is anger a virtue?

A. When anger is not self-centered

B. When anger is used in behalf of others' welfare

C. When anger is tempered with compassion — v. 5

5. A Good Day for Doing Good. (3:1-6). A popular slogan today is "Have a good day." Sunday is a good day not only for having a good day, but for doing good. Jesus implied this when he asked, "Is it lawful on the sabbath to do good . . . ?" Sunday is a good day to do good — how so?

A. Do good to God by worship — Jesus was in the synagogue — v. 1

B. Do good to others by helping — Jesus healed — v. 5

C. Do good to self by getting spiritual food — 2:23-24

Illustration

Laws, Laws, Laws!
A few years ago Congress considered some 15,000 bills. Approximately 500 were passed into law. During the same year 250,000 bills were introduced in state legislatures. About 50,000 of them became laws. Every citizen has approximately 1,500 laws to obey.

Sabbath Laws.
The sabbath law forbid work on the sabbath. The scribes had thirty-nine different types of labor that were forbidden. Under each type there were additional rules dealing with details. Some of them:
— Shoes with nails were not to be worn, for the nails would be a burden and no burden weighing more than two dried figs was allowed.
— No fire was to be lighted on the sabbath.
— An egg could not be boiled.
— A woman was not allowed to look in a mirror on the sabbath lest she discover a grey hair and be tempted to pull it out.
— Plucking grain was forbidden because it was a kind of reaping and the rubbing off of the husks was the work of threshing.
— If a man was bitten by a flea, he was compelled to let it bite lest he be guilty of the sin of hunting on the sabbath.
— In the event of sickness, one could do what was necessary to keep the person from getting worse, but not that which would make the person better.
There were at least 1,500 ways of breaking the sabbath law.

Outdated Laws.
— There is a New York law forbidding blind men from driving an auto.
— A Kentucky law requires every person to take a bath at least once a year.
— New York City has a law requiring the whiskers of Santa Clauses to be fireproof.
— In Seattle one is not allowed to carry a concealed weapon over six feet in length.
— There is a law in Nicholas County, West Virginia, forbidding clergy from telling funny stories in their sermons.

The Need for Anger.

Whoever is without anger, when there is cause for anger, sins.
— St. John Chrysostom

In an address to the students at the University of Michigan, Lee Iacocca said:

I want you to get mad about the current state of affairs. I want you to get so mad that you kick your elders in their figurative posteriors and move America off dead center. Getting mad in a constructive way is good for the soul — and the country.

Justified Anger.

A young man working for a major oil company was transferred to the main office in Chicago because he was something of a whiz kid. The president called him in and told him there was a rich oil field near Purcell, Oklahoma. It was on a ranch where the owner had died. He explained, "There's going to be a public sale of the oil and gas rights on this property. We don't think anyone knows about the oil. I don't want you to think it is too important, but if you don't get the rights, don't come back."

The young man caught a train that would arrive in Purcell at 4:10 a.m. Knowing that he was a heavy sleeper, he called the porter, gave him a twenty dollar bill, and said, "Porter, I need your help. I've got to get off this train in Purcell at 4:10 a.m. I am a very heavy sleeper, and may not want to get up, but see that I do." The porter replied, "I used to play professional football. I'm sure I can handle it."

The next morning, about 7:30, the porter and conductor were having a cup of coffee when all of a sudden the door burst open. The young man, still in his pajamas, grabbed the porter, shook him, and threw him into a chair. Later the conductor said, "I believe that is the maddest man I've ever seen." The porter explained, "You should have seen the fellow I put off this morning at Purcell."

Another Healed Hand.

Jeroboam, king of Israel, offered a sacrifice on an altar he had built before golden bulls. A prophet from Judah preached that God would raise up Josiah and destroy the altar and the priests. King Jeroboam stretched forth his arm and pointed to the prophet and said, "Seize that man!" At once his arm was paralyzed and he

79

could not bring it back. The altar fell apart. Jeroboam pleaded with the prophet to pray for him and asked for the healing of his arm. The prophet prayed and the arm was healed. As a reward, the king asked the prophet to come to his palace and have something to eat. The prophet refused and returned home. (1 Kings 13:1-10).

A Promise for Obedience.
The Lord says,

> If you trust the sabbath as sacred and do not pursue your own interests on that day; if you value my holy day and honor it by not traveling, working or talking idly on that day, then you will find the joy that comes from serving me. I will make you honored all over the world, and you will enjoy the land I gave to your ancestor, Jacob. I, the Lord, have spoken.
>
> (Isaiah 58:13-14)

A Carpenter Saves Seamen

The Miracle
of Stilling
a Storm

Mark 4:35-41

(Matthew 8:23-27; Luke 8:22-25)

Pentecost 5

On that day, when evening had come, he said to them, "Let us go across to the other side." ³⁶And leaving the crowd, they took him, just as he was. And other boats were with him. ³⁷And a great storm of wind arose, and the waves beat into the boat, so that the boat was already filling. ³⁸But he was in the stern, asleep on the cushion; and they woke him and said to him, "Teacher, do you not care if we perish?" ³⁹And he awoke and rebuked the wind, and said to the sea, "Peace! Be still!" And the wind ceased, and there was a great calm. ⁴⁰He said to them, "Why are you afraid? Have you no faith?" ⁴¹And they were filled with awe, and said to one another, "Who then is this, that even wind and sea obey him?"

A tour group, forty of us consisting of Christian laity, pastors, bishops and their spouses, came one morning to the Sea of Galilee. The sky was blue, the wind was calm, and the waves were lazily coming to shore. Our plan was to board a boat crossing the lake to visit a Jewish settlement on the east side of the Sea. The boat looked safe and the weather was perfect. No one had any hesitation to go aboard. When about a mile from shore, a strong wind came up and soon the boat was ploughing through waves. The storm became more severe, and the waves became ten feet high. It was a double-decker boat with an exposed top floor for better observation. Several of us were up there holding on as the boat fell and rose with each wave. All of a sudden a huge wave came and sent a wall of water over us, leaving us drenched. Needless to say, many were frightened and worried that the boat would sink. Fortunately, the power motors pushed us to the other side of the lake, and we were thankful! Some were heard to say, "If I had known it was going to be that rough, I'd never have boarded the boat. You will never get me on a boat again to cross the Sea of Galilee!"

If a large, motor-driven boat was tossed about by a sudden storm on the Sea of Galilee, think of what a small boat for thirteen men with only a sail to propel it would do in a similar storm in Jesus' day. How much more frightened they must have been than we were! They had no motor, no life jackets, no short-wave radio to call for help.

Jesus was with the Disciples when the storm came. After they awakened him, he commanded the wind and waves to be calm. They were saved from destruction and death. When we compare our experience on the lake with the Disciples, why did we Christians, in the name of Jesus, not still the storm and assure our safety? Indeed, the Disciples had Jesus with them. We also had Christ in our hearts. Does it mean that Christ no longer saves people in natural catastrophes? Does Jesus save us today only in mental, emotional, spiritual and psychological storms that threaten our lives? Or, is this only an interesting nature story that has no relevance to today's storms? These and other questions will cause us to struggle as we prepare a sermon on the miracle when a Carpenter saved a group of seamen from drowning.

Acclimation

The Setting.
The miracle, of stilling the storm, comes at the end of chapter 4. It follows a series of parables.
Mark 4:35-41 is the first of a series of mighty works of Jesus:
1. Power over the sea — stilling the storm — 4:35-41
2. Power over demons — Gerasene demoniac — 5:1-20
3. Power over disease — Healing of a hemorrhaging woman — 5:24b-34
4. Power over death — Jairus' daughter — 5:21-24a, 35-43

The Situation.
It was at the end of a busy day for Jesus: teaching a mass of people, arguing with the scribes and explaining the parables to the Disciples. To get away from the crowd and to get some rest, Jesus suggested they go across the lake, a distance of eight miles. He was dead tired and soon fell asleep on a pillow at the stern of the boat. While he was asleep, a storm came up. The winds caused the waves

to enter the boat and it was almost swamped. In terror, the Disciples shook Jesus awake and asked him if he did not care that they were all about to drown. Jesus stood up and addressed the wind, "Be quiet!" After he said the same to the waves, there was a great calm. Then Jesus looked at his terrified Disciples and asked, "Why are you frightened? Where is your faith?" They had no answer, but with deep reverence and awe, they asked among themselves, "Who is this that even the wind and waves obey him?"

The Parallel Passages (Matthew 8:23-27; Luke 8:22-25).
1. The three Evangelists report different names the Disciples used for Jesus: Matthew, "Lord"; Mark, "Teacher"; Luke, "Master, Master."
2. Items only in Mark's account:
A. They took Jesus in the boat "just as he was" — v. 36
B. Other boats accompanied Jesus' boat — v. 36
C. The Disciples asked an accusatory question: "Do you not care?" — v. 38
D. Jesus was "in the stern, asleep on the cushion" — v. 38
E. In rebuking the wind and water, Jesus said, "Peace, be still!"
3. Points of agreement:
A. Jesus was asleep during the storm
B. The boat was in danger of sinking
C. The Disciples were frightened
D. Jesus rebuked the wind and sea
E. Jesus questioned their faith.
F. The Disciples marvelled at Jesus' power over nature.

The Lectionary (Pentecost 5).
Lesson 1 (2 Samuel 5:1-12). David is crowned king of Israel and establishes his reign in Jerusalem. Just as David conquered his enemies, the Jebusites, someone greater than David is king over the wind and waves, as described in today's Gospel Lesson.
Lesson 2 (2 Corinthians 5:18—6:2). God, in Christ, reconciled the world to himself and gave to the church the ministry of reconciliation. Reconciliation signifies that peace has come between God and sinners. "Therefore, since we are justified by faith we have peace with God . . ." (Romans 5:1)
The relation to the Gospel Lesson: Jesus says to the storm: "Peace! Be still!" The storm and the boat were enemies. Jesus reconciles the two and calm results.

83

Gospel (Mark 4:35-41). The Gospel Lesson continues our journey through Mark. Today's pericope is the second of two selections from chapter 4. Next Sunday we will begin reading from chapter 4 for two more miracles. Today's Gospel points to the amazing power Jesus had over the forces of nature. This, in turn, focuses our attention upon Jesus as one who has the power of God.

Explanation

Sea (vv. 39, 41).

The Sea of Galilee is really only a good-sized lake, thirteen miles long, eight miles wide, and 680 feet below sea level. It is a fresh water lake fed by the waters from northern mountains, such as Mt. Hermon, whose snow-topped peak can be seen from the Galilean Sea. The water flowing from the lake creates the Jordan River, which flows into the Dead Sea, a super-salty lake in which nothing lives.

Storm (v. 37).

For a lake so small, one may wonder how a life-threatening storm could be a problem for experienced boaters. The sea seems to lie in a valley with mountains on both sides. Unexpectedly, winds from beyond the mountains come and swoop down, creating an effect much like an air tunnel. This causes the waves to become turbulent, threatening the small boats on the lake.

Wind (v. 37).

The wind has terrific power. A hurricane can lift more than sixty million tons of water, and can generate more power every ten seconds than all the electric power used in the United States in a year. One look at the devastation left by a hurricane convinces one of the mighty power of the screaming wind. The wind stirs up the water and makes mountainous waves. When Jesus was awakened, he first spoke to the wind. When it died down, the sea became calm. When the wind is calm, the sea is as still as a mountain lake.

Rebuked (v. 39).

Jesus rebuked the wind and the waves as though they were evil. In the Old Testament, the sea is often the symbol of chaos and opposition to God. Accordingly, there is no sea in heaven.

(Revelation 21:1) The ferocious wind and powerful waves were like demons bent on human destruction. The material elements are treated as evil powers over which Jesus has control. When one is caught in a severe storm and life is threatened, it is easy to think of the wind and waves as enemies out to kill. Jesus rebuked the demons of wind and wave, as he had rebuked the demon in the possessed man (Mark 1:25) and the fever in Peter's mother-in-law. (Luke 4:39)

Just (v. 36).

The Disciples took Jesus in their boat "just as he was." What does this mean? They took him improperly dressed for a boat trip? Was he hungry? Exhausted? Did they want him to be other than he was? What did they want him to be? Yet, Jesus must always be accepted not on our terms, but only on his terms — just as he is.

Perish (v. 38).

This is no idle word, nor a hyperbole. The Disciples were scared to death that they would drown. These men were experienced and seasoned fishermen who knew all about boats and how to handle them — the water did not easily frighten them. But the storm was terrific. Waves came into the boat. It was about to be swamped. They had no life jackets. There was no ship-to-shore radio with which to send an SOS call. It was dark. And back there was their leader fast asleep!

Faith (v. 40).

Jesus asked the Disciples if they were scared because they had no faith. Faith in what or in whom? Faith in themselves? Faith in their boat? Faith to stop the storm? Faith will not stop a natural disaster. Paul's faith did not prevent a shipwreck. Faith will not keep a plane from falling. What did Jesus mean by asking if they had faith? Was it not faith in him as lord of creation — faith that he could and would protect them from disaster? When a storm strikes, we are naturally frightened at the prospect of death, but faith in Jesus overcomes the fear, as we put our trust in his power and grace.

Sleep (v. 38).

Lying on the stern with a pillow for his head, Jesus sleeps during the storm. How would anyone sleep when the boat was tossed around like a cork, with the sail whipping around, and twelve passengers screaming with fear? His sound sleep may have resulted from two things. One, he was physically exhausted after a day's teaching and healing with the crowd. It reminds us how human he was. Second, he was at peace with God. His conscience was clear and good. He was right with his Father.

Awe (v. 41).

The men were filled with awe at Jesus. Here is a man who removes a killer storm by simply telling the wind to calm down. They were amazed, astounded and flabbergasted. They had to ask, "Who is this man?" They had been associated with him for months, day and night, but no one had dreamed that this Jesus was in control of nature. They must have asked, "Could this man be the Messiah?"

Application

Relevance of Revelation.

1. *"Who Then is This?"* This question, asked by the Disciples, is still a question in our day. What human being can with a word stop a hurricane or a tornado? Naturally this leads us to ask who this man is. If a man has control of natural forces, is he not more than a man? The miracle of stilling the storm gives us another picture of Jesus. We have so domesticized him to be only human, a brother and friend, that he is a limited person. The miracle shows us a Jesus who has in his hands the power of creation and who commands obedience. Here is a Jesus full of glory and power. It is this concept that is needed in our day to counterbalance the popular Jesus, meek and mild.

2. *The Storms of Life.* Is the miracle of stilling the storm on the Sea of Galilee just a nature narrative? It may be interesting, but it is historical and objective. We are not likely to get caught in a storm on the Galilean lake. There is a possibility of getting caught in a hurricane, tornado, earthquake or snow storm. But even then, we do not believe that if we have faith in Jesus, the storm will end. To make the storm applicable to our lives, is it wrong to allegorize or spiritualize the storm? Are there not personal storms of stress, of sorrow and of tragedy? In these storms, is it not true that faith in Christ can bring calm and peace?

3. Fear and Faith. In the miracle, the Disciples were frightened and Jesus asked where their faith was. Fear and faith are always with us, then as now. Faith is the cure for fear. But, that raises questions about today's storms and our faith. We know that faith will not stop a storm. It is not faith in general, but faith in Christ. We believe that he has the power to save. We believe he cares enough to save us. We may not be rescued from the storm and may even perish in it, but by faith we commit our souls into his hands for safe keeping.

Sermon Suggestions.

1. Storms Are Natural. Storms are a part of life. They are inevitable. No one can escape the storms of life, whether a physical or a personal storm. Even Jesus was caught in a storm at sea. Though the Disciples had Jesus with them, they experienced a storm. Just because we are Christians, we have no reason to expect skies always blue and winds always mild. The sermon can help people to know what to do when storms come and how to survive them.

2. Faith Has No Fear. Faith may not have fear, but it does have trouble, storms and peril. Faith may not remove the storms of life. Faith in Christ does remove fright because there is trust in Christ's power and grace to deliver us safely from the storm. Even if we perish in the storm, we have no fear of death, for Christ is there to gather us into his loving and secure arms.

3. Does Jesus Care? Why did the Disciples think Jesus did not care about their safety? He was sleeping while they were struggling to stay alive! How would anyone sleep with such turbulence and noise and confusion? There are times when we are in difficulty, and God is silent and seems to be absent. We pray, but we get no answer. Where is God? Does he not care about our plight? Physically, Jesus was asleep and not aware of their predicament. Spiritually, Jesus never sleeps and is constantly concerned about his people's welfare. The Psalmist assures us, "Behold, he who keeps Israel will neither slumber nor sleep." ((Psalm 121:4)

4. Who Is This Man? The stilling of the storm focuses upon the man who said to the wind, "Peace, be still!" No other human could make natural forces obey. Can this man be God incarnate, the Messiah? The Disciples understood a new dimension of this man who ate and slept with them. Obviously, he was more than a teacher and preacher. If he had power over nature, was there nothing he could not do? Yet, with all that power at his disposal, he refused to use it to save himself on the Cross.

5. *Just As He Is.* We sing, "Just as I am." We ask Jesus to take us just as we are. But, do we take Jesus "just as he is?" The Disciples took Jesus from the beach where he was teaching into their boat. He was tired and worn out. He was sleepy. He was not dressed for a boat trip. Some, today, have trouble taking Jesus just as he is. They want only a human Jesus, a teacher, a good storyteller, a miracle man. But they will not take him as God's Son, the Savior. Or, they want the divine Jesus only. We may want the Jesus who blesses children, but not the Jesus who drives out moneychangers in the temple.

6. *Saved by Association.* In the account of this miracle, we see the value of association. In one case, the Disciples were associated with Jesus in the boat. If he had not been with them, they would have drowned. Even if Jesus had not awakened, do you think God would have allowed his Son to drown? Because God took care of his Son, those associated with him were also saved.

Then there is the case of the other boats that left at the same time as the boat with Jesus. (v. 36) Since the boats were together, they faced the same peril as the Disciples' boat. When Jesus stilled the storm, the other boats profited by the calm. They, too, were saved by their association with Jesus.

7. *Peace and Peril.* During the storm, the Disciples had no inner peace. Though they were experienced and expert seamen, they were frightened as they faced a watery death. Is it possible to have peace in the midst of peril? It is possible, if we have Christ with us by faith. Jesus is our peace. He is the prince of peace. As Paul said, because we are justified by faith, we have peace with God. Peril may be external to us, but peace can be an internal possession resulting from trust in God's grace and power.

Sermon Structures.

1. *A Time for Questions (vv. 35-41).* When trouble comes and disaster threatens, it is normal for people to ask questions. In the miracle, pivotal questions are asked, questions that need answers.
   A. Don't you care, Jesus? — v. 38
   B. Why are you afraid? — v. 40
   C. Who then is this? — v. 41

2. *When Storms will not Go Away (vv. 35-41).* Physical and psychological storms are a part of life. Having faith does not stop the storms. What can Christians do while the storms rage?

A. Have the comfort of Jesus' presence — v. 36

B. Be assured of Jesus' love and concern — v. 38

C. Have faith in eternal life — v. 40

3. Fear — Before and After Christ (vv. 35-41). In the story of the storm there are two experiences of fear by the Disciples:

A. A negative fear: scared of possible death — v. 38

B. A positive fear: awe, amazement, respect — v. 41

4. Who's Who (v. 41) Who is this man who can command the wind and waves to obey him? When we want to learn the identity of a person, we consult, *Who's Who in America.* We consult the Gospels for the answer to the Disciples' question.

A. An exhausted human — "asleep" (v. 38)

B. A man with divine power — "rebuke" (v. 39)

C. A teacher of faith — v. 40

5. How to Sleep without Sleeping Pills (vv. 35-41). The sale of sleeping pills is big business because many have trouble going to sleep. Counting sheep is not enough! Without the benefit of a sleeping pill, Jesus was sound asleep in spite of a topsy-turvy boat, a whistling wind and terrified men. It is possible to follow Jesus in his example of sleeping:

A. Take Jesus with you to bed — "just as he was" — v. 36

B. Accept his peace — v. 39

C. Trust his protection and deliverance — v. 40

6. The Value of Association (v. 36). By association we reap the benefits of others. We do nothing to deserve the benefits. For the sake of those with whom we are associated, we receive blessings. This was the situation during the storm at sea.

A. The Disciples' association with Jesus — "They took him." (v. 36) If they had been alone, they would have perished.

B. The other boats' association with Jesus' boat — "Other boats were with him." (v. 36) The additional boats were in the same storm, and they were saved by the same miracle.

7. Peace can be Yours (v. 39). There may be a storm in your life. You are confused, bewildered, and downright scared. What or who can quiet you and cause you to relax? The prince of peace says, "Peace, be still."

A. When you are tied up in knots of nerves — stress

B. When you are scared of what might happen — fear

C. When you are concerned about health or livelihood — worry

Illustration

Association.

A farmer planted a cornfield near a marsh. As the corn was ripening, flocks of cranes began to fly in to plunder his grain. The angry farmer set a trap in the field. The next day he caught a large flock of cranes and among them was a stork. He began to kill the cranes, but when he came to the stork, it protested vehemently, "You cannot kill me! Can't you see I am a stork, not a crane, the most devout of birds?" (the ancient Greeks considered the stork to be partly sacred.) The farmer replied, "You may be a stork, the most devout of birds, but if you fly with cranes, you die with cranes!"

At a county fair, a farmer entered his old, skinny farm horse to run in a race with beautiful and strong race horses. His friends asked him, "Why in the world did you enter your old nag when you knew she could never win a race?" "Well," the farmer explained, "I entered her because I thought that the association would do her some good."

Faith Gives Assurance.

In his *Letters and Papers from Prison* (p. 162) Dietrich Bonhoeffer wrote:

I must be able to know for certain that I am in God's hands.
Then everything becomes easy, even the severest privation. It
is a matter of my facing everything in faith.

Christ Cares.

A father was teaching his son to ride a bicycle. The boy said, "Dad, I'll never be able to do it. Look at all my friends, why they can ride in circles and everything." His dad told him to forget what other kids could do and to just learn to ride with his father holding on. As the two practiced daily, the boy began to realize that his father cared. By his actions he seemed to be saying, "I'll look after your happiness, security, success, all you need. I'll take care of you."

Peace Through Caring.

A group of businessmen were having dinner with Archbishop Desmond Tutu, the 1984 Nobel Peace Prize winner and leader against South Africa's apartheid. As they were finishing their dessert, one

90

asked Tutu what they could do to promote world peace. Archbishop Tutu gazed into the distance and thought for a moment. Then in a quiet voice he answered, "You must care."

God Asleep?

In his movie, *Love and Death*, Woody Allen tells his adored Sonya, "If God would only speak to me — just once. If he would only cough. If I could see a burning bush or the seas part . . ."

Power of Nature.

In December 1988, a very severe earthquake hit Armenia, Russia. The casualties were: 50,000 dead, 130,000 injured and 500,000 homeless.

Fear Has Power.

The late Dr. Raymond deOvies, dean of St. Philip's Cathedral in Atlanta, told about his experience. One evening his mother sent him on an errand. He decided to take a short cut across a cemetery. Not watching where he was going, he stumbled over a pile of dirt and fell into an open grave. He jumped as high as he could, but he always fell back. Finally he decided to wait for help. It was not long before he heard someone whistling as he approached. He recognized it as his old friend, Charley. Then suddenly there was a cry, a sliding sound, and a thud. Charley had fallen into the same hole. It was so dark that Charley could not see Raymond, slumped back in the shadows. Charley, too, tried to get out, but couldn't. Finally Raymond could resist the temptation no longer. In a deep sepulchral voice he growled: "Can't you leave a man in his own grave in peace?" The reaction was electric. Charley was up and out of there as if he had wings!

Problem of Sleep.

It is estimated that fifty million Americans have a problem with sleep. One-third of the population has trouble going to sleep. They take twenty-one million sleeping pills every night to go to sleep. Thirty-one million prescriptions for sleep are written each year. Americans spend annually one billion dollars for sleeping aids.

Life For The Dead
And Dying
Two Healings

Mark 5:21-43

(Matthew 9:18-26; Luke 8:40-56)

Pentecost 6

When Jesus had crossed again in the boat to the other side, a great crowd gathered about him; and he was beside the sea. [22]*Then came one of the rulers of the synagogue, Jairus by name; and seeing him, he fell at his feet,* [23]*and besought him, saying, "My little daughter is at the point of death. Come and lay your hands upon her, so that she may be made well, and live." And he went with him.*

A great crowd followed him and thronged about him. [25]*And there was a woman who had a flow of blood for twelve years,* [26]*and who had suffered much under many physicians, and had spent all that she had, and was no better but rather grew worse.* [27]*She had heard the reports about Jesus, and came up behind him in the crowd, and touched his garment.* [28]*For she said, "If I touch even his garments, I shall be made well."* [29]*And immediately the hemorrhage ceased; and she felt in her body that she was healed of her disease.* [30]*And Jesus, perceiving in himself that power had gone forth from him, immediately turned about in the crowd, and said, "Who touched my garments?"* [31]*And his disciples said to him, "You see the crowd pressing around you, and yet you say, 'Who touched me?'"* [32]*And he looked around to see who had done it.* [33]*But the woman, knowing what had been done to her, came in fear and trembling and fell down before him, and told him the whole truth.* [34]*And he said to her, "Daughter, your faith has made you well; go in peace, and be healed of your disease."*

[35]*While he was still speaking, there came from the ruler's house some who said, "Your daughter is dead. Why trouble the Teacher any further?"* [36]*But ignoring what they said, Jesus said to the ruler of the synagogue, "Do not fear, only believe."* [37]*And he allowed no one to follow him except Peter and James and John the brother of James.* [38]*When they came to the house of the ruler of the synagogue, he saw a tumult, and people weeping and wailing loudly.* [39]*And when he had entered, he said to them, "Why do you make a tumult and weep? The child is not dead but sleeping."* [40] *And they laughed at him. But he put them all outside, and took the child's father and mother and those who were with him, and went in where the child was.* [41]*Taking her by the hand he said to her, "Talitha cumi"; which means, "Little girl, I say to you, arise."* [42]*And immediately the girl got up and walked (she was twelve years of age), and they were immediately overcome with amazement.* [43]*And he strictly charged them that no one should know this, and told them to give her something to eat.*

It happens almost every day. We hear a screaming siren, and see red lights flashing, and a speeding car. If we are on the same road, the law requires us to pull to the side and stop. As it whizzes past us, we see it is an ambulance rushing to the site of an accident or taking a person to a hospital before the person dies. A devout Christian says a silent prayer on behalf of the injured or sick one.

Suppose one would flag down the ambulance and say, "Wait, there is a sick lady here that needs your attention." Do you think the paramedics would stop, get out of their car, and minister to a woman with a chronic bleeding problem? Indeed, they would not even stop, but would rush on to help the dying person. The merely sick woman could be helped at a later time.

A similar situation occurred in Jesus' day. He received a summons from a distraught father to come to his house at once to heal his twelve-year-old dying daughter. Immediately Jesus goes with Jairus, the father. The crowd that assembled to welcome Jesus off his boat went along. As the crowd was jostling along, a woman with a twelve-year-old bleeding problem sneaked up behind him and touched his robe. At once Jesus stopped and asked who had touched him, for he felt power leave him. With the touch she was healed, but when Jesus picked her out of the crowd, she surrendered and explained why she had touched him. After sending her home in peace, Jesus resumed his fast walk to help the dying girl. But by this time she was dead, and the funeral custom was already in progress. Jesus stopped the mourning and went to the room of the dead girl, took her by the hand, and raised her to life.

This would not happen today. An ambulance would not stop for a lesser illness when another person was dying. But then, today one would not get healed by the touch of a holy man's garment or be brought back to life by the touch of a hand and a word from his lips. Nevertheless, the story teaches us that Christ has the power of God to overcome disease and death, then and today.

Acclimation

The Setting.

Mark continues to give illustrations of Jesus' power. Last Sunday his power over the storm at sea was demonstrated. Now we enter the fifth chapter of Mark and read about three other evidences of his power, power over three of humanity's greatest enemies:

1. *Demons* — vv. 1-20
2. *Disease* — vv. 25-34
3. *Death* — vv. 21-24, 35-43

The Situation.

Jesus and his disciples returned to the west bank of the Sea of Galilee near Capernaum. They are met by a large crowd. Among them is Jairus, the lay leader of the local synagogue.He prostrates himself before Jesus, begging him to come to his house to heal his little girl of twelve, who is dying. Accompanied by the crowd, Jesus goes with Jairus to heal the girl. As they are on their way, a woman suffering from a twelve-year hemorrhage, who had tried all the doctors and got no help, and who had spent all her money, joins the crowd thinking, "If I could just touch his clothes, I will be well." When she does, her bleeding stops. Sensing that power has left him, Jesus asks who has touched him. The Disciples think this a foolish question, because they are so crowded that touching others is unavoidable. But Jesus looks around to see who it was. The woman, conscience-stricken, comes to him and explains everything. He assures her that her faith has made her well and dismisses her with his peace.

During this exchange with the woman, a messenger reports to Jairus that his daughter has died and that therefore it is no longer necessary to trouble Jesus. Jesus ignores the message and urges Jairus not to be frightened, but to have faith. He dismisses all except Peter, James, John and Jairus, and they continue to Jairus' home. When they arrive, there is a tumult of weeping and wailing by professional mourners. Funeral music is provided by flute players. Jesus asks them why they are crying, for he claims that the child is not dead but sleeping. Being certain that the child is dead, they laugh at him. He orders all out of the house, and takes the parents and the three Disciples into the room where the child lies. Jesus takes her hand and says in Aramaic, "Talitha cumi," "Little girl, arise!" At once she arises and walks around. This amazes them. The experience ends with Jesus ordering them not to tell about the miracle and to give the girl something to eat. Then Jesus goes to Nazareth, his home town.

The Parallel Passages: (Matthew 9:18-26; Luke 8:40-56).

1. Points of Difference:

A. The child. In Mark and Luke, Jairus tells Jesus that his daughter is at the point of death, but Matthew reports, "My daughter has just died." Only Luke tells us that she was his only child. Mark and Luke tell us the girl was twelve years old.

B. Jairus. He was the ruling official of the Capernaum synagogue. His humility and acknowledgment of Jesus' greatness was expressed in Mark and Luke by his falling at Jesus' feet, but Matthew has him only kneel.

C. The crowd. In Matthew there is no crowd that goes with Jesus to Jairus' home. Consequently, Matthew does not tell of Jesus' question, "Who touched me?" In Mark and Luke there is a crowd going to the home and a crowd in the home mourning the dead girl.

D. The raising. Only Mark uses the Aramaic words, "Talitha cumi." Matthew has Jesus say nothing; he only takes the girl's hand. Mark and Luke report that Jesus ordered the parents to give the girl something to eat.

E. Flutes. Only Matthew reports that there were flute players at the home of the deceased.

2. Points of Agreement:

A. Jairus, a leader of the synagogue, in a show of humility, begged Jesus to come to his home to heal his twelve-year-old daughter, who was near death.

B. While Jesus was on his way to help Jairus' daughter, a hemorrhaging woman touched him and was healed.

C. By the time Jesus arrived at Jairus' home, the girl was dead. Nevertheless, Jesus claimed she was sleeping, not dead. For this claim, the mourners laughed at him.

D. Jesus brought the child back to life and all were amazed.

The Lectionary.

Lesson 1 (2 Samuel 6:1-15). This lesson is one of a series on the life of David. It concerns the bringing of the ark of the covenant from Baalah to Jerusalem. To keep the ark from falling off the cart when the oxen stumbled, Uzzah touches the ark and is killed for his irreverence. Frightened, David leaves the ark with a Philistine. When David hears that the ark has brought blessings to Obed Edom, he returns and brings the ark to Jerusalem with a great celebration.

95

The relation to the Gospel miracles: in the case of the ark and Uzzah, we see the power of God. A touch brought death. In contrast, the power of God's Son was life through a touch. The bleeding woman received life by touching Jesus' garment. The little girl received life out of death when Jesus took her by the hand.

Lesson 2 (2 Corinthians 8:7-15). In this pericope, one of a series from 2 Corinthians, Paul appeals to the Corinthian church to respond financially to the appeal for the relief of poverty and hunger in Jerusalem. Jesus is the example of one who became poor to make them rich. So, they are to share their riches with the poor.

The relation to today's Gospel: in the two miracles we see Jesus giving health to a sick woman and life to a dead girl. Out of love and compassion he is ever giving himself to others. In the case of healing the bleeding woman, he felt power leaving him when she touched his garment. In the miracles, Jesus gives more than gold; he gives the most precious gift of all — life.

Gospel (Mark 5:21-43). Today's Gospel lesson gives us two miracles: the healing of the hemorrhaging woman and the raising of Jairus' daughter. If the Gospel is used for the text of the sermon, isn't there too much ground to cover? In the Lutheran Lectionary,this Gospel is divided into two miracles. Thereby a preacher may choose one or the other miracle. Though the Common Lectionary calls for both miracles, it is still possible to choose one or the other. Another possibility is to use as a text the entire Gospel, because the two miracles are very closely interrelated. The one occurs within and in connection with the other. The two miracles illustrate common elements:

A. Need. Both miracles illustrate the urgent need of the persons involved. They did all they could. They were at the point of despair. The bleeding woman had consulted doctors for twelve years and spent all her money on doctor bills and medicines, but to no avail. The girl was at the point of death, and no one could help her get well. As a last resort they turned to Jesus.

B. Touch. The healings involved Jesus' touch. He touched the girl by taking her hand and raising her up. The woman touched Jesus' garment. Through the touch the life-giving power of health and life came to the afflicted.

C. Faith. In both cases, faith was an essential to healing. In the case of the woman, Jesus said, "Your faith has made you well." When it was announced that the girl had died, Jesus urged Jairus to "only believe."

96

D. Dying. In both miracles there was the existential fact of death. When Jairus came to Jesus, he reported that his daughter was dying. Before they could reach her home, she died. The woman with the issue of blood was experiencing a slow death. For twelve years she had been losing blood, not normally for one week a month, but day after day, each day of the month for twelve years. In her time, blood transfusions were not available. She was in the process of bleeding to death. In both cases Jesus saved them from death.

E. Daughters. The two miracles deal with daughters. The twelve-year-old girl was the only daughter of Jairus. She was a daughter by natural birth. In the case of the bleeding woman, Jesus addressed her as "My Daughter." She was his daughter by the adoption of grace.

F. Power. In both miracles Jesus' power of life and health is demonstrated. Because of his compassion, he goes to Jairus' home to heal the girl. His power over death was in his words, "Talitha cumi." In the case of the woman, his power went from him when she touched his clothes. With her touch came immediate healing. Because of Jesus' love for people, the very power of God was used only for good, life, and health.

Explanation

Ruler (v. 22).

Jairus was one of the rulers of the synagogue in Capernaum. As a ruler, he was the lay leader of the congregation and was responsible for the services and for the maintenance of the property. As a ruler, he was a prominent person in the community and was held in high regard and respect. In the light of this, we can appreciate his humility and earnestness when he fell at Jesus' feet. This occurred when he saw Jesus get off the boat. What did he see in Jesus? Other religious leaders saw Jesus as one in league with Satan, or one who was insane, or a blasphemer. In contrast, Jairus saw in Jesus a man of compassion and power. Probably he had seen Jesus heal others in his synagogue and thereby had confidence that Jesus could heal his critically ill daughter. Jairus was a respected religious leader, a man of humility, a lover of his family and a person appreciative of Jesus' concern for the needy.

Blood (v. 25).

The unnamed woman in the crowd was ailing. For twelve years she had had a continuous flow of blood, day after day, year after year, for twelve years. According to Leviticus 15:25-27, a woman with this problem was considered ritually unclean. Anything she touched, such as a bed or a chair, was also made unclean. She was not allowed to attend synagogue and not permitted to associate with others. She was not to touch another person or to be touched. Simply by being in the crowd, she was breaking the law. This explains why she went to Jesus secretly, and why she wanted to touch only his garment.

Well (vv. 23, 28, 34).

The woman wanted to touch Jesus' garment that she might be well. Jairus asked Jesus to lay his hands on his dying daughter that she might be well. The Greek word, *sozein*, is used. It means to be saved, made whole or made healthy. Illness was considered the result of disharmony with God. To be saved is to be rightly related to God. As a result, the person would be whole, well or healthy.

Power (v. 30).

When the woman touched Jesus' garment, he felt power leaving him. The healing took something out of him as he gave himself to her. As God's Son, he had God's power, which was demonstrated in the miracles. He was like a power transformer which can be heard to hum with power. A transformer reduces the tremendous power of the powerhouse so that it can be used locally. The infinite power of God the Father was reduced and made applicable to a person. The miracles were like flashes of lightning revealing God's omnipotence. This power did not come by magic or incantations, but by the simple word of God, such as "I say to you, arise!"

Fear (v. 32).

The reaction to the woman's healing was fear. When Jesus saw who had touched him, the woman came forward and explained. Why did she come with fear and trembling? Why not with joyful gratitude? She knew she had done wrong. She had broken the law by coming into the crowd and making many ritually unclean by her touch. She had gotten her healing on the sly. Instead of asking Jesus for help, she had slipped behind him and stolen his blessing. She was conscience stricken. Would Jesus rebuke her or take away the healing? Would the authorities imprison her for breaking the law? Her fear was dissolved when Jesus commended her for her faith.

Tumult (v. 38).

Jesus described the situation in Jairus' home as a "tumult." Friends and neighbors crowded the house to express sympathy. There was weeping and wailing. As the custom was, professional mourners and flute players were hired to express grief. The poorest family was expected to hire at least two professional women-mourners and one flutist. Since Jairus was probably a wealthy man, many additional mourners and musicians were present. The people rent their clothes and tore their hair to express their grief. The place was bedlam.

Daughter (vv. 23, 34).

In these miracles there are two daughters, one twelve years old, another with a twelve-year-old malady. The one was a natural daughter born to Jairus and his wife. As his only child, she was precious to her father, who prostrated himself in total humility to persuade Jesus to heal her. Here is a daughter born of the flesh but dearly loved. The other daughter, the woman, belonged to Jesus by adoption. The New English Bible and the Good News Bible have Jesus say not "Daughter" but "My daughter." By her faith in him, he accounted her as his child in the Kingdom. Through baptism, believers receive adoption as the daughters and sons of Christ.

Faith (vv. 34, 36).

Jesus urged Jairus not to fear, but to "only believe." He answered the woman that her faith had made her well. This faith is not the popular "faith healing" which may produce healing through the power of suggestion. Faith does not heal, for, as in the case of the paralytic, there was the faith of others. Faith is not directed to Jesus, but to the power of God which Jesus uses. Faith is the human response to God and opens up the self for God's power to heal and save. Yet, faith is not only passive, but active, in seeking God's favor and help.

Sleeping (v. 39).

The crowd of mourners in Jairus' home had a "good" laugh when Jesus told them there was no need of their weeping since the child was sleeping. If this were literally true, the mourners had a case. They knew the child's heart was no longer beating and that her body was cold and stiff. Also, if "sleeping" is taken literally, there was no miracle of raising one from the dead. Of course, Jesus knew she was dead, but he viewed death as a sleep. Sleep implies there will be an awakening to life beyond death. We go to sleep on earth and we awaken in heaven.

Arise (v. 41).

Taking the girl by the hand, Jesus tenderly but authoritatively says, "Little girl, I say to you, Arise!" Jesus brings the child back to life. This is not a true resurrection, for the child will still die at some future date. It is a case of resuscitation. Resurrection is the rise of life out of death to die no more. Resurrection is the new life known as eternal life. Christians who died with and in Christ also rise with Christ to life everlasting. The miracle of raising the girl declares that Jesus has the power to conquer even death.

Application

Relevance of Revelation.

1. Power for the Powerless. Today many feel powerless to do anything about themselves and their life situations. What can one person do about the tense international situation with its poverty, hunger and injustices? What can a single person do about a national scandal involving drugs, sexual license and greed? What can I do about a terminal illness or the approaching death of a loved one? In a time like this, it is assuring to know of One who has power to overcome disease and death. By faith in Christ we have God's power to overcome the world. Today's two miracles are relevant to those who are helpless by giving them hope and assurance of victory in Christ. The miracles assure us that nothing is too hard for God. His power is at our disposal so that "I have the strength to face all conditions by the power that Christ gives me." (Philippians 4:13)

2. Miracles for Today? We have no trouble believing that when Jesus was on earth, a touch of his garment could heal, and his touch and word could bring a person back to life. But what of today? We cannot expect Jesus to do these miracles today through the church. These things just do not happen today. In that case, what message do these miracles have for us? Shall we allegorize or spiritualize them? Indeed, Christ still heals and cures diseases, but he uses different methods today. It does no good to stand beside a casket and say, "In the name of Jesus, arise." No, but Christ gives us courage and hope in dying because of his gift of eternal life. In the two miracles before us, we find eternal truths that can help us in our pilgrimage.

3. Women and Children. The miracles of today's Gospel Lesson concern two females, an adult and a twelve-year-old girl. In today's society many women are battered by husbands and too many children suffer physical, mental and sexual abuse by parents. Although the woman in the miracle was not a battered woman and the girl was by no means abused by her father, the subject of women and children can be related and involved in sermons on these miracles. Christ would relieve women of suffering and would want all children to be loved and cared for.

Sermon Suggestions.

1. Give God a Chance! In both miracles there was a desperate need. The woman for twelve years had gone from doctor to doctor and gotten nothing but bankruptcy. Jairus had tried everything to make his daughter well, but she was dying. We turn to Christ at the point of utter despair. In our time we have very serious problems of alcoholism, drugs, greed, crime and moral corruption. We have tried legislation, education, and materialism. Still there is no cure. It is time to give God a chance to heal a sick society.

2. Whose Girl are You? When a child is very small, a parent playfully may ask, "Whose girl (boy) are you?" The parent would smile and give a hug when the child said, "Daddy's" (Mommy's). In the miracles we have two daughters. Jairus had a natural daughter; Jesus had an adopted daughter ("My daughter" — v. 34) One was by the first birth; the other was by a second birth. Everyone had a physical father, but everyone should have God as Father.

3. Two Ways to Die. The miracles show that there are at least two ways to die. The little girl had a quick death. Before Jairus and Jesus could get to her, she had died. And how early she died — twelve years old! The bleeding woman was experiencing a slow death. For twelve years she had been losing blood. Transfusions at that time were unknown. She was not only isolated because of her ritual uncleanness, but she was eventually going to bleed to death. Both deaths are serious and final. Jesus has power to overcome both kinds of death. For a Christian, one type of death is the sudden one of martyrdom; the other is a slowly burning out by self-giving service.

4. Story Sermons. Both Jairus and the bleeding woman are excellent subjects for story sermons. Either or both can be subjects of stories in terms of biographical sermons. We can tell about Jairus, the religious man, a loving father and a believer in Jesus' power to help. The woman's story deals with her embarrassing need, her isolation, her devious method to get help and her open confession.

5. A Two-way Touch. Many telephones are now touch phones. We press buttons and we "reach out and touch someone." The two miracles involved touching. Jesus touched the dead girl and raised her to life. So we sing, "He touched me . . ." The bleeding woman reached out to touch Jesus' garment and was healed. This was not an isolated incident, for Luke reports, "All the people tried to touch him, for power was going out from him and healing them all." (6:19) A touch works both ways: Christ touches us or we touch Christ.

6. Feeling Drained? When the woman in the miracle touched Jesus' mantle, he felt the loss of spiritual strength. When we help people, we are often emotionally drained because we have given of ourselves. Sermons drain preachers who pour themselves into their messages. This raises the question of what is going from our lives. What is taking your life's blood out of you? Is it fear, worry or anxiety? Or, is it a worthy expenditure? Every time we help or do good, it takes something out of us, even as power left Jesus.

7. Interruptions. It seems that someone always calls for help when we are busy. We are interrupted in what we are doing at the time. This was the case with Jesus' going with Jairus to heal his daughter. On the way, a woman stopped him and got healing. He held up the march to Jairus' home to help a suffering woman. Why couldn't she have waited until he cured the girl? Jesus could have said, "I'll see you later. I must hurry, for a child is at the point of death." The lesson is that Jesus is never too busy to heed our cries for help. He wants to be interrupted in order to help us.

Sermon Structures.

1. A Miracle Within a Miracle (vv. 21-43). The text gives two miracles, one within the other. This sermon is designed to discuss the common elements in both miracles.

A. The urgent need — vv. 23, 26

B. The presence of faith — vv 34, 36

C. The touch of life — vv. 28-29, 41

2. From a Nobody to a Somebody (vv. 24b-34). In the healing of the hemorrhaging woman, there is a progression from her being a nobody to a somebody, from an outcast woman to a beloved daughter.

A. A nobody — v. 25 (No name, isolated, a woman, diseased)

B. An anybody — v. 31 (In the crunch of the crowd, anybody might have touched Jesus. The woman was an anybody.)

C. A somebody — v. 34 ("My daughter")

3. No Greater Power (vv 30, 41). Jesus claimed that all power was given to him in heaven and on earth. This power was seen in the healing of a woman and the raising of a child. The physicians lacked the power to heal the woman, and no one could bring a dead person back to life. Today there is even a greater power than seen in these miracles. Christ's power is seen at its best.

A. The power to save a soul from death

B. The power to turn a sinner into a saint

C. The power to live a victorious life

4. A Father-daughter Affair (vv. 23, 34). In the two miracles there are two fathers and two daughters. Every person, son or daughter, can and should have two fathers.

A. A natural daughter born of the flesh — v. 23 (The need of a father like Jairus — loving, caring.)

B. An adopted daughter born of the Spirit — v. 34 (Jesus claims her as "My daughter.")

5. A Two-way Touch (vv. 28, 41). In a day when we have touch telephones, touch typewriters and touch computers, life seems to be one touch after another as we go through a day. Both miracles of this Sunday result from touching.

A. The touch of faith — v. 28 (The woman's touch of Jesus brought immediate healing.)

B. The touch of life — v. 41 (Jesus took the girl by the hand and raised her out of death.)

6. The Last Laugh (v. 40). Though Jesus had a sense of humor, the Gospels do not report that Jesus ever laughed. He is known as a man of sorrows. Though he may not have laughed, he was laughed at, as in the case of the mourners in Jairus' home. They may have laughed, but Jesus had the last laugh when Jesus was laughed at in derision.

A. Laughed at for his teaching — death is a sleep — v. 40

B. Laughed at as a king — Roman soldiers — Matthew 27:27-31

C. Laughed at while on the Cross — Mark 15:29-30

Illustration

Urgency.

A bumper sticker says, "GOD BLESS AMERICA — and please hurry." The motto of our age is "Keep moving." We do not want to wait for anything. Jairus' appeal to Jesus was to come quickly, for his daughter was dying.

Need for God's Help.

A minister was appalled at the language of one of the barbers where he went for a haircut. His language was most vulgar and obscene. One time he noticed the absence of the barber and inquired about him. He was told that he had been very ill and almost died. Some time later, the minister was getting his mail at the Post Office and he heard his name called by someone in an automobile. He went to the car and found that it was the profane speaking barber. With a weak voice the barber said, "Preacher, I want to tell you something. I was in a coma at the hospital. I could not move or see, but I could hear. I heard the doctor tell my wife that I could not live another hour. I never prayed in my entire life but I prayed then, 'O God, if there is a God, I need you now.' " With tears he said, "I've kicked God in the face every day of my life for sixty years. And the first time I called his name, he came."

A Stolen Blessing.

In a sneaky way the bleeding woman slipped up behind Jesus and touched his garment and was healed. An anonymous writer says the same about the thief on the cross:

> *Say, bold but blessed thief,*
> *That in a thrice*
> *Slipped into paradise,*
> *And in plain day*
> *Stol'st heaven away,*
> *What trick couldst thou invent*
> *To compass thy intent?*
> *What arms?*
> *What charms?*
> *Love and belief.*

God Heals Through Physicians.

The woman in the miracle who went to doctor after doctor, received no help for her hemorrhaging and spent her last dollar on doctors' fees. Today God can help through medical doctors. Albert Schweitzer went to Lambarene, Africa to be a medical missionary. When his patients awakened from the anesthesia, the first words they heard were from Schweitzer: "The reason you have no more pain is because the Lord told me to come to the banks of the Ogowe."

Being a Somebody.

The woman in the miracle was a nobody until Jesus made her a somebody by calling her his daughter. John Cheever was aware of his fame in his home town of Ossining, New York. One time someone stopped him on the street and said, "You're David Wayne, the actor." "No, I'm not," said Cheever. "Well, who are you?" Cheever answered, "I'm somebody." "So am I," the stranger replied.

Touch of Life.

Jesus' touch is a touch of life. His touch brought life to the little daughter of Jairus. This is to be expected of God's Son, our Lord Jesus. In the Sistine Chapel Michelangelo painted the creation of Adam. God is shown reaching out to Adam, and with a pointed finger touches the finger of Adam. Then, according to Genesis, Adam became a living soul.

A One-Word Miracle
The Healing of
a Deaf Mute

Mark 7:31-37

Pentecost 16

Then he returned from the region of Tyre, and went through Sidon to the Sea of Galilee, through the region of the Decapolis. ³²And they brought to him a man who was deaf and had an impediment in his speech; and they besought him to lay his hand upon him. ³³And taking him aside from the multitude privately, he put his fingers into his ears, and he spat and touched his tongue; ³⁴and looking up to heaven, he sighed, and said to him, "Ephphatha," that is, "Be opened." ³⁵And his ears were opened, his tongue was released, and he spoke plainly. ³⁶And he charged them to tell no one; but the more he charged them, the more zealously they proclaimed it. ³⁷And they were astonished beyond measure, saying, "He has done all things well; he even makes the deaf hear and the dumb speak."

It all happened with a single word! It was like pressing a button that releases, like the button you press to open your car's glove compartment or the hood of your car. The "magic" word was *Ephphatha*. It must have been so impressive that Mark records the original Aramaic word, the native language of Jesus. However, this one word was probably not heard by the patient, for he was stone deaf. But, at the saying of the word, his ears were opened and his tongue was released to enable him to speak clearly. One little word did it!

The word was "Open." The man's ears were so tightly shut that he could not hear. His tongue was tied by the inability to hear words. He is the representative of many today who are uptight with stress, worry, anger, fear and hatred. To get release some turn to tobacco, alcohol, drugs and sex. Many fill the offices of psychiatrists.

Christ gives us openness. A business often has a sign, "OPEN," in the front window or door. Likewise, Christians could hang a sign around their necks saying "Open." When we worship, we pray,

"O Lord, open thou my lips." (Psalm 51:15) An opening hymn says, "Open now thy gates of beauty." Christ sets before us "an open door." (Revelation 3:8) To express his openness to his people, Paul writes, "Our mouth is open to you, Corinthians; our heart is wide." (2 Corinthians 6:11) The Cross was an opener. The veil before the holy of holies in the temple was split in two, and the way to God was opened by the Cross. At the time of Jesus' death, an earthquake shook the earth and graves were opened. Easter, too, was an opening experience. The women coming to the tomb wondered who would open the tomb for them. An earthquake occurred and the stone was rolled away. (Matthew 28:2) Forgiveness is release from the prison of sin and attains openness to God. Since God wills openness for his people, Christ performs a miracle to open the ears and release the tongue of a nameless man, the subject of today's miracle.

Acclimation

The Setting.

Jesus felt the need to get away for a while from the mad pace of his ministry in Galilee. Opposition was mounting. King Herod was watching him. The common people wanted to make him their king. He leaves the country for the seacoast towns of Tyre and Sidon. According to Mark, his seclusion was interrupted by a Canaanite woman's appeal to heal her demon-possessed daughter. Later he takes his Disciples to Caesarea Philippi, which is in the same northern territory, for the crucial question, "Who do you say that I am?"

In chapters 7 to 9 Mark tells of a change in Jesus' ministry. Heretofore it was to the nation. Now it is semi-public. In the light of his impending doom, he specializes on the training of the Twelve as preparation for his Passion.

For today's miracle we find that Jesus has returned to the Sea of Galilee by way of Decapolis. He is confronted by a group of people asking him to heal a deaf man with a speech problem.

The Situation.

Upon Jesus' arrival at lake Galilee, some people begged Jesus to heal a man who could not hear or speak clearly. In response to their appeal, he took the man away from the crowd and dealt with him privately. Jesus put his fingers into the man's ears, put saliva on his finger and then touched the man's tongue, looked up to heaven, sighed, and said in his native tongue, *Ephphatha,* "Open up!" At once the man was able to hear and speak plainly. There is no recorded response on the part of the man. Although Jesus ordered the people not to say anything about the healing, in their amazement they had to tell, saying, "He does everything well . . . ."

Comparative Translations.

Verse 31 — RSV uses "Decapolis"; GNB — "Ten towns."

Verse 32 — RSV says "They brought"; GNB explains "they" as "some people."

Verse 32 — "Impediment" in RSV becomes in GNB "could hardly speak."

Verse 32 — RSV uses "besought"; KJV — "beseech"; Phillips — "begged."

Verse 33 — RSV says Jesus "spat and touched his tongue"; Phillips — "touched his tongue with his own saliva."

Verse 34 — RSV — Jesus "sighed"; GNB — "deep groan."

Verse 34 — RSV translates *Ephphatha* "Be opened"; GNB — "Open up."

The Lectionary (Pentecost 16).

Lesson 1 (Proverbs 2:1-8). This pericope calls upon us to seek the wisdom of God. We are to beg for knowledge and insight. The result of doing so is to have the fear of the Lord and to learn about him. In relation to the miracle in the Gospel Lesson, it suggests that we should be open to wisdom.

Lesson 2 (James 1:17-27). This is the first of four selections from the book of James. We are admonished not only to hear, but to do the Word of God in terms of personal purity and social action. A possible connection with the Gospel Lesson: Before we can do the Word of God we must first hear it, calling for open ears. One way of doing the Word is to help someone who is handicapped and hurting as the deaf man was.

Gospel (Mark 7:31-37). After an excursus of five Sundays on John 6, the lectionary resumes our study of Jesus' ministry recorded in Mark. Today's Gospel is the second selection in the resumed series that takes us to the end of the church year. The subject of today's Gospel, recorded only in Mark, is the miraculous healing of a deaf man with impaired speech. Mark considered the miracle a fulfillment of messianic prophecy. "The blind will be able to see, and the deaf will hear. The lame will leap and dance, and those who cannot speak will shout for joy. (Isaiah 35:5-6)

The theme of the passage is based on Jesus' word, *Ephphatha,* "Be opened" — the opening of the ears to hear and the loosening of the tongue to speak. Little is known about the man, his name, family, work, faith, response. The focus is upon the miracle.

A. The people's part — v. 32
B. The privacy — v.33
C. The use of non-verbal language — vv. 33, 34
D. The word of healing — vv. 34, 35
E. The people's reaction — vv. 36, 37

Explanation

Decapolis (v. 31).

It is a Greek word meaning "Ten Towns"; the Decapolis was a confederation of free cities in a region east of the Jordan River. Jesus returned from northern seacoast towns to the Sea of Galilee via the Decapolis.

Brought (v. 32).

The deaf man did not come to Jesus on his own accord. He was brought by some people who were concerned for his welfare. Since he was deaf, it is possible that he had not been aware of Jesus or what he could do. Even if he had come to Jesus on his own, his speech was so garbled that he could not be understood. The people felt sorry for this man because his affliction isolated him, ruined the possibility of social conversation and probably affected his employment. It points to the need for people to bring others to Jesus for healing and salvation.

Impediment (v. 32).

It was not that the deaf man could not speak. His problem was that he could not speak plainly so that he could be understood. His speaking problem was related to his lack of hearing. We learn pronunciation from hearing others speak. A deaf person cannot hear their own sounds. Today many learn from radio and TV reporters and commentators how to pronounce unfamiliar names such as

109

Gorbachev, Dvorak, chrysanthemum, etc. Dictionaries and encyclopedias give charts of symbols for correct pronunciation, but correct pronunciation depends ultimately upon hearing. First Jesus healed the man's hearing and then the man spoke plainly.

Hand (v. 32).
The people requested Jesus to lay his hand upon the afflicted man. The laying on of hands was synonymous with healing. It was the touch of healing which Jesus frequently used. The hand was the physical contact through which the healing power went from Jesus to the suppliant. The laying on of hands has spiritual significance also. By the laying on of hands, the Holy Spirit is given. Examples include baptism, confirmation and ordination.

Indeed, Jesus used his hands to heal this man. He put his finger in his ears and touched his tongue. Surely, Jesus could have healed him without these contacts, but since the man was deaf, he used nonverbal language to communicate with the man. It was a case of body language. We communicate by posture, gestures, facial expressions, tone of voice, eyes, etc. In New Zealand there is a type of dog that corrals sheep, not by barking, but only by the use of eyes.

Spat (v. 33).
Why did Jesus spit before he touched the man's tongue? He spit not in the man's face or in his mouth. He spit to get saliva. In Jesus' day saliva was regarded as remedial. It was a sign of soul power. We can see Jesus spit into his hand, and then with saliva on his fingers, he touched the tongue of the deaf man. Later Jesus used the same method when he healed a blind man: "After spitting on the man's eyes . . ." (Mark 8:23)

Privately (v. 33).
Wherever Jesus went, there was a crowd who heard what he had to say or witnessed a healing. In this case, Jesus took the man away from the crowd so that the two of them could be alone. Why did he do this "behind closed doors"? It may have been for Jesus' sake. He did not want publicity as a wonder-worker. He did not want a following based on his ability to heal. He was in the world primarily for spiritual purposes, to reveal God's nature and to reconcile the world to God. He was more concerned about soul, than body healing. Or, the privacy may have been for the man's sake in order to

avoid embarrassment. A deaf person with defective speech was always in a situation that caused people to gawk or to comment. By doing it privately, Jesus eliminated people's talk about the man and the miracle. To avoid embarrassment today, we do not refer to a person as "deaf and dumb" but as one who has a hearing disability and a speech difficulty.

Sighed (v. 34).

After touching the man's ears and tongue, Jesus looked to heaven for help and then sighed. This was not the only time he sighed. Another instance was when the Pharisees came to him wanting to see a miracle. Mark reports: "He sighed deeply in his spirit . . ." (Mark 8:12) What was the meaning of this sigh? Was it an expression of weariness and exhaustion? Was there no end to healing person after person? Was he frustrated by dealing with physical problems when he wanted to deal with spiritual needs? As Jesus looks at us and our condition, does he sigh saying, "What am I going to do with these people?"

Ephphatha (v. 34).

This is a treasured word, because it is a word used in Jesus' own language, Aramaic. It is similar to the Aramaic words used when he raised Jairus' daughter, *Talitha cumi.* (Mark 5:41) Mark translated the word for us, "Be opened" or "Open up!" The man's ears were shut, blocked and closed so tightly that he could not hear. His tongue was tied, and he could not speak plainly. Was this order, "Be opened," spoken to the man, to the organs or to demons? Was the cure physical, emotional, psychological or a combination of all three? Openness implies that the man was tense and a victim of stress. He was tied up in knots. When he let go and relaxed, his hearing came back and then he could hear how to pronounce words. When we are uptight, tighter than a drum, there are physical repercussions. This may have been the case with the deaf man.

Application

Relevance of Revelation.

1. Release from stress. Today many suffer from stress leading to burn-out. Stress is one of the major problems in today's society.

We are living at such a mad pace that we get uptight, nervous and paralyzed with fear and worry. For some, life is one big headache. Children in school are under stress to get top grades. Men are under stress to be successful in business. Women have the stress of two careers: motherhood and business. Crisis experiences have built-in stresses. As a result, we resort to sedatives and tranquilizers and seek psychiatric help. If only we could push a button that would cause us to unwind! In today's miracle Jesus points to the deaf man's problem: "Be opened!" This infers that the tension was released and the ear could now hear and the tongue could speak. Christ is the button we may push for relief and release from stress.

2. *Spiritual Openness.* What good is this story of a deaf man's healing for people today in the same condition? Is it possible to go to a school for the deaf and preach this miracle ending with *Ephphatha*? If we had enough faith, would all the deaf get back their hearing? Is there a person that would expect this to happen? Has it ever happened in twenty centuries of Christian preaching? This miracle speaks to a far greater problem, spiritual openness. We are manacled by our sins and need release through forgiveness. We suffer from deafness to God's message to us. Consequently, we do not know how to speak plainly to God.

3. *Open Ears but Closed Minds.* There are two kinds of deafness. We may not hear because of physical or psychological impairment. There is a far larger group of people who have perfect physical ears with wonderful hearing. Jesus had his problem with the latter group. "He who has ears, let him hear." (Matthew 11:15) The trouble is that people with good ears to not hear because they do not want to hear. Others hear but do not listen. This is a daily, continuing problem for us. We often ask, "Do you hear what I am saying?" or "Listen to me!" To those with good ears Jesus says today, "Open up your ears!" How does one do this? When we go to Christ and accept him by faith, our ears will open. But what does it mean to go to Christ and accept him?

Sermon Suggestions.

1. Before You Speak. We usually say, "Think before you speak." As in the case of the deaf man, we must first hear before we can speak. The man's speech became clear after he was able to hear. If we do not hear how words are pronounced, we cannot properly speak them. In Clara Scott's hymn, "Open My Eyes That

I May See," we pray for open ears, before we pray for open mouths. In his first letter, John gives the same order: "that which we have seen and heard we proclaim . . ." (1 John 1:3) Unless we first hear the Word, we have nothing to communicate. Witnessing is producing by hearing.

2. *Plain Talk.* When the string of the deaf man's tongue was cut, "he spoke plainly." The problem for us is not necessarily faulty enunciation or pronunciation. Rather, our problem is double talk. We hedge on issues. We love to use our professional jargon or legalese. When we are finished, no one seems to know what we were talking about. The time has come to tell it as it is — no evasion of the issues, no inuendos. Plain talk says that a sin is a sin, death is death, and crime is crime. There is no sense in "beating around the bush"; we must speak the plain truth.

3. *How People Get to Jesus.* Usually we do not come to Jesus on our own steam. Some people brought the deaf man to Jesus. Similarly, four men carried a paralytic for healing. Andrew brought Peter to Jesus. When we were baptized as infants, our parents brought us to Jesus. Recent studies reveal that a majority of new church members come to Christ through the influence of friends and/or neighbors. To bring people to Jesus calls for faith in Jesus on our part. We must believe that Jesus is the answer to people's needs. Moreover, to bring people to Jesus calls for loving them. Apparently the people felt sorry for the deaf man. They loved him enough to want healing for him. Evangelism is the church's program for bringing sinners to the Savior based upon our faith in Jesus and love for people.

4. *A Private Healer.* Jesus took the deaf man away from the crowd so that they could have some privacy. The average miracle worker, like a magician, would want the crowd to see his fantastic power. This was not for Jesus. He wanted no publicity. Healing was a side issue for him. He was more concerned about healing souls than bodies. In addition, Jesus must have taken into consideration the feelings of the handicapped man. Probably he would have been embarrassed as the center of attention. Getting away from the crowd meant, also, that there were no interruptions nor distractions. This private healing shows us that Jesus was interested only in helping a man and not in his own reputation or notoriety. He is not only a "wounded healer" but a private healer.

5. *Body Language.* Jesus faced a problem of communication with the deaf man. They left the crowd and the two were alone. Since

the man could not speak plainly, how could Jesus explain his need? Moreover, if Jesus spoke to him, he could not hear what was said. In the light of this, Jesus had to use non-verbal communication, sign language as is done today. Only Jesus had a different set of symbols for communication. First, he put a finger in the man's ears, then a finger with saliva on the man's tongue, and then he looked to heaven. What was Jesus saying to the man? The ear was to hear, the tongue was to speak, and the power to do this came from above. When Jesus said, *Ephphatha*, did the deaf man hear the word, or did hearing return after the command? How we act, how we react, and how we live speak more effectively than our words.

6. *One Little Word will Heal Him!*. In Luther's "A Mighty Fortress" he speaks of the power of a word in opposing Satan. One line says, "One little word shall fell him." Likewise, one little word from Jesus performs a miracle, just one word — *Ephphatha*, an Aramaic word. It is a word that commands one to relax, to let go, to "let it all hang out," and to let your hair down. One is to be as relaxed as an empty potato sack. Perhaps this was a psychosomatic case. The man was so uptight that he could not hear, and because he could not hear, he could not speak clearly. With this one word, release came and he opened up. It points to the power of divine words. At Creation, the universe came into being when "God said, Let there be light, and there was light." The Word of God is truth, life and power. It behooves us to hear and inwardly digest the Word for the opening of our lives to love and truth.

7. *Not One, but Two*. At this miracle, Jesus faced not one speech problem, but two. In the one case, Jesus was called upon to enable a man to speak plainly. The man could not communicate or be understood. The other case was the opposite. Jesus ordered the people to say nothing about the healing, but the more he discouraged them, the more they broadcast the news. Their refrain was, "He has done all things well." Did the people forget this on Good Friday when they screamed, "Crucify him!"? It is a problem for us, too. There is a time when we have nothing to say when we ought to speak. And there is a time when we should remain silent but don't!

Sermon Structures.

1. *Open Up! (vv. 34-35)*. People can have closed minds and hard hearts. If so, they are self-centered and living within themselves. Like the deaf man, they cannot hear, nor communicate. They are isolated

in their own little worlds. To be open means to be able to receive God's blessings. The following come from God to those who are open:

    A. Open to faith

    B. Open to truth

    C. Open to love

    D. Open to the Holy Spirit

2. A Totally Open Person (vv. 31-35). Christ would want everyone to be a totally open person. He indicated this in the healing of the deaf man. The whole person needs to be open for the fullness of Life.

    A. Open eyes — look to heaven for help — v. 34

    B. Open ears — to hear God's Word — v. 33

    C. Open mouth — to praise, think, witness — v. 33

3. Release Me and Let Me Live Again! (v. 34). To be open is to be released from fear, worry and hatred. To be open is to be delivered from self-centeredness, selfishness and pride.

    A. Release *from*: stress, worry, fear, hatred

    B. Release *to*: live, love, serve

4. Bring as You were Brought (v. 32). Some people brought the deaf man believing that Jesus would and could heal the man. If they had not brought him, he probably would not have been healed. Usually people do not become believers in Christ, and thus do not receive the benefits of faith, by themselves. Family and/or friends brought us to Jesus. How can we bring others?

    A. Bring people to Jesus through prayer

    B. Bring people to worship services

    C. Bring children for baptism

    D. Bring people by loving them into the Kingdom

5. How to Get Released (vv. 31-37). It is easy to say, "Relax. Take it easy. Stop your fretting and worrying." The person wants to be released from tension and nervousness. The big question is how to get release, how to be open.

    A. Look to heaven in faith — "looking up to heaven"

    B. Let Christ enter — "into his ears," "touched the tongue"

    C. Love neighbor and self — "He has done all things well"

6. Hear ye! Hear ye! (vv. 31-37). This miracle of healing a deaf man is compared with good news. it tells us much about Jesus.

    A. His compassion by healing — Jesus loves you

    B. His power to heal — Jesus can save (heal) you

    C. His fulfillment of Messianic prophecy — Jesus is your Savior

Illustration

The Pain of Deafness.

The doctors told Beethoven, "You will hear less and never again." In response to this tragic report, the famous composer wrote:

My misfortune is doubly painful because it must lead to my being misunderstood, for me there can be no more recreation in the society of my fellows, refined intercourse, mutual exchange of thought, only just as little as the greatest needs command may I mix with society, I must live like an exile.

Non-verbal Communication.

Jesus used non-verbal communication with the deaf man. He used body language of eyes, ears and mouth. Albert Mehrabian tells of a study in communications that says most of our communication is by body language: seven percent is communicated by words; thirty-eight percent by tone of voice; and fifty-five percent by body language such as posture, gestures, facial expressions, etc.

Help from Heaven.

Before healing the man, Jesus looked up to heaven as the source of his power to heal. It was reported to King Jehoshaphat that three armies were converging on Jerusalem. He and his people were frightened. He called a national fast, and called the people to assemble in the temble for prayer. He himself led the prayer,

O our God, wilt thou not execute judgment against this great multitude that is coming against us. We do not know what to do, but our eyes are upon thee.   (2 Chronicles 20:1-12)

Have to Tell.

The more Jesus charged the people not to tell about the miracle, the more they shared it. It was too good to keep it to themselves. Two boys and a little brother were playing ball. One hit the ball into a window. They looked around to see if anyone had seen what happened. No one had seen it except the little brother. They asked him not to tell anyone. He refused to say he would not. The big brother offered him a ball if he would not tell. It was refused. Then he offered him a new baseball glove, but the little fellow would not cooperate. Then he was offered a baseball bat. This, too, was refused. In exasperation the older brother asked, "What do you want not to tell?" The little lad shouted, "I wanna tell!"

116

The Meaning of Openness.

*The opening of doors is a mystic act: it has in it some flavor
of the unknown, some sense of moving into a new moment,
a new pattern of the human rigmarole. It includes the highest
glimpses of mortal gladness: reunions, reconciliations, the bliss
of long-parted lovers reunited. Even in sadness, the opening
of a door may bring relief: it changes and redistributes human
forces.* — Christopher Morley

No Distractions.

The miracle was done privately probably because there were no
distractions or interruptions, and because both could concentrate.
It is said that when Leonardo completed *The Last Supper*, he asked
a friend to inspect it and give his opinion about it. After looking
at the now-famous painting for a long time, the friend said, "That
goblet is wonderful. It stands out like solid silver." At once da Vinci
took his brush and with one stroke wiped it off the canvas. Then
he explained, "Nothing shall draw the eye of the beholder from my
Lord."

Open Ears to Truth.

A closed mind will not hear truth. Open ears are necessary to
receive the truth of God. The American Bible Society tells of
Sirithone, who at age twenty entered a Buddhist monastery in
Thailand. He became a priest and studied Buddhism for nine years.
To become a missionary to the West, he needed to learn how to speak
English. He walked several miles each day to a Christian missionary
who agreed to teach him English. Their textbook was John's Gospel.
As the monk learned English, he also learned about Christ, and faith
began to develop in him. In defiance of his family and friends, he
became a Christian, left the monastery and today he is a Christian
pastor in Thailand. Miracles can happen when ears are open to the
gospel truth.

117

Prelude to Passion

The Healing of Blind Bartimaeus

Mark 10:46-52
(Matthew 20:29-34; Luke 18:35-43)

Pentecost 23

They came to Jericho; and as he was leaving Jericho with his disciples and a great multitude, Bartimaeus, a blind beggar, the son of Timaeus, was sitting by the road-side. [47]*And when he heard that it was Jesus of Nazareth, he began to cry out and say, "Jesus, Son of David, have mercy on me!"* [48]*And many rebuked him, telling him to be silent; but he cried out all the more, "Son of David, have mercy on me!"* [49]*And Jesus stopped and said, "Call him." And they called the blind man, saying to him, "Take heart; rise, he is calling you."* [50]*And throwing off his mantle he sprang up and came to Jesus.* [51]*And Jesus said to him, "What do you want me to do for you?" And the blind man said to him, "Master, let me receive my sight."* [52]*And Jesus said to him, "Go your way; your faith has made you well." And immediately he received his sight and followed him on the way.*

Do you remember when as a child you played the game, "Blind Man's Bluff"? Someone blindfolded you, turned you around several times to confuse you, and then you were to catch someone. All was black as coal. You stumbled into this and that. With outstretched hands you tried to touch someone. The other players kept out of your reach lest they be the next one to be blindfolded. It was a very upsetting experience for you, but an hilarious one for those who watched you grope and stumble.

It was far worse to be blind in Jesus' day than it is today. There were no schools or homes for the blind. The blind did not have Braille for reading, nor cassettes, nor radios. Then the blind had no white canes or seeing-eye dogs. There were no verbally interactive computers. The blind in Jesus' day had little or no help. Since a blind person could not see to work, they had to sit on the sidewalk and beg for food. It was a life of extreme poverty and social isolation.

On Jesus' last journey to Jerusalem, he and his followers pass through Jericho. A blind man, Bartimaeus, hears the commotion and asks what is going on. When he learns that Jesus is passing by, he realizes that this is his opportunity to become cured of blindness. With all his might, he cries for mercy. He refuses to be silenced, for he realizes that this is his last chance. It is now or never, a life of darkness or light. His persistent appeals cause Jesus to stop and ask for him to come forward. Throwing down his robe, Bartimaeus goes as fast as he can to Jesus. When Jesus asks him how he can help him, without hesitation, he asks for his sight. Bartimaeus is given his sight and Jesus explains that his faith has made him well. Then Bartimaeus joins the crowd and follows Jesus to Jerusalem.

This was Jesus' last miracle before entering Jerusalem on Palm Sunday. It was the prelude to the Passion. His public ministry came to an end with the giving of sight to a blind man.

Acclimation

The Setting.

With a large crowd of sympathizers, Jesus and his Disciples are on their way to the Passover celebration in Jerusalem. It was his final trip to the holy city. On the way he and the multitude pass through Jericho. Here Jesus performs his last miracle of healing on a blind man, Bartimaeus. It is also the last miracle in Cycle B of the Lectionary.

The Jericho story ends the section, 8:27—10:52. Mark 11 has Jesus in Jerusalem and his triumphal entry is described. (11:1-10) The Jericho experience served as a prelude to the passion history.

The miracle was preceded by the request of James and John to have the chief seats of authority in Jesus' Kingdom. Like Bartimaeus, they were blind to the nature of the Kingdom and the meaning of discipleship. While Bartimaeus was physically blind, the sons of Zebedee were spiritually blind and therefore in need of a similar miracle.

In this miracle the focus is not on Jesus, but on Bartimaeus. He was the center of attention, which he gained by his persistent shouting for mercy, his refusal to be silent, his immediate response to Jesus' call, and his following Jesus to Jerusalem. In this miracle Jesus does not touch to heal and gives no command to heal. Jesus simply announces, ''Your faith has made you well.''

119

The Situation.

The time has come for Jesus to make his last offer to his nation to be her Lord and Savior. With a large crowd of supporters and his Disciples, Jesus makes his final journey to the capital city. On the way he goes through the ancient town of Jericho. As the crowd walks, Jesus talks with the people and answers their questions. A blind man, Bartimaeus, is at his customary place begging because his blindness prevents him from holding a job. He hears the shuffling of hundreds of feet and the voices of people. Something unusual is happening, and he wonders what is going on. He asks, and someone tells him that Jesus is passing by. At once, at the top of his voice, he shouts, "Jesus, Son of David, have mercy on me!" His repeated yelling disturbs people trying to hear what Jesus is saying. They berate him and tell him to shut up. In defiance, he cries out even more loudly and finally gets Jesus' attention. Jesus stops the procession and tells the people to bring the blind man to him. At this good news, Bartimaeus can't wait to get to Jesus. He throws off his mantle, jumps up, and goes as fast as a blind man can to Jesus. When he arrives, Jesus asks him what he wants him to do for him. Bartimaeus answers, "Teacher, I want to see again." Without touching his eyes, without praying for healing, without a command that the blindness should disappear, Jesus simply says, "Go, your faith has made you well." At once Bartimaeus could see. Then he joined the crowd going with Jesus to Jerusalem.

The Parallel Passages (Matthew 20:29-34; Luke 18:35-43).

1. The Number of Blind Men. Matthew has two blind men, while Mark and Luke have only one. Mark alone gives his name, Bartimaeus.

2. The Town of Jericho. Matthew tells us that the miracle occurred as Jesus and the crowd were leaving Jericho. Mark has them in the city. Luke says they were entering the town.

3. The Call to Bartimaeus. Matthew has Jesus call the blind men and ask, "What do you want me to do for you?" Mark and Luke say that Jesus asked the people to bring Bartimaeus to him. In this case Jesus calls Bartimaeus through his associates.

4. The Touch. In Matthew Jesus touched the eyes of the blind men and they received their sight without Jesus' saying, "Receive your sight." There is no healing by touch in Mark and Luke.

5. The Mantle. Only Mark tells us that the blind man threw off his garment and ran to Jesus. This shows his eagerness to be healed.

6. The People's Reaction. Only Luke reports that when the people saw the miracle, they praised God for it.

7. Points of Unanimity.

A. A great crowd accompanied Jesus as he passed through Jericho on his way to Jerusalem.

B. A blind man (men) sat on the roadside begging.

C. The blind cry for mercy in the name of the Messiah, "Son of David."

D. Jesus asked the same question, "What do you want me to do for you?"

E. The blind receive(s) sight.

F. The blind follow(s) Jesus.

The Lectionary (Pentecost 23).

Lesson 1 (Jeremiah 31:7-9). We often refer to Jeremiah as the weeping prophet who had to speak the Word of God in terms of doom and destruction for the nation. He foretold of their captivity in Babylonia because of their sins. It broke his heart to have to say these dreadful things. However, in this passage Jeremiah speaks of hope and God's promise to bring back the people and restore the nation. At that time there will be rejoicing, singing and dancing. Probably, this lection was chosen because of its reference to the "blind" (v. 8), in relation to the healing of blind Bartimaeus in the Gospel Lesson.

Lesson 2 (Hebrews 5:1-6). This pericope is the fourth in a series of eight from the book of Hebrews. It speaks of God's appointment of Jesus as the eternal high priest after the order of Melchizadek. In relation to the healing of blind Bartimaeus, we can see Jesus, the high priest, interceding for Bartimaeus and succeeding in getting God's power to restore his sight. The function of a priest is to intercede for hurting people that they might be blessed. This happened when Jesus, by God's power gave sight to blind eyes.

Gospel (Mark 10:46-52). Today's pericope is a transition from Jesus' public ministry to his ministry in Jerusalem during the last week of his life (Holy Week). It happened on the threshold of his triumphant entry into Jerusalem (Palm-Passion Sunday). Here was a blind man who seized the opportunity to be healed as Jesus was passing through his city. He was a man who would not take "No" for an answer. His persistent cry for help caught Jesus' attention. He was a man who had not sight, but had insight into the identity

121

of Jesus as Messiah. He was a man who knew what he wanted and needed, sight. At the end he was a man who was so filled with gratitude that he became a follower of Jesus.

Explanation

Jericho (v. 46).

Jericho is a small town fifteen miles from Jerusalem and five miles east of the Jordan River. It is a lovely town of many palm trees, good water supply and prolific gardens. It is situated in a valley. From the top of Mt. Nebo, the city can be seen in the distance. It is like a green garden, an oasis in a desert, surrounded by treeless mountains and brown, grassless terrain. Jericho is an ancient city. When the Israelites crossed the Jordan to enter the Promised Land, Joshua instructed his people to march around the walls until, on the seventh day, they fell. The walls of blindness also fell for Bartimaeus when Jesus healed him.

Bartimaeus (v. 46).

He is the only patient named in Mark. His name means "Son of Timaeus." Because he was blind, he had to beg to live. We are not told whether he had a family. At the time of Jesus' passing through the city, he was the man of the hour. He was a man of faith in Jesus, a persistent fellow, a man who knew what he wanted. When he got it, he followed his benefactor as a disciple.

Blind (v. 46).

Bartimaeus was a blind person. Was he born blind? Was he blinded by a disease or accident? According to Luke's account, Bartimaeus says to Jesus, "I want to see *again*." (v. 41, emphasis mine) Though he was physically blind, he had spiritual insight, for he recognized the Messiah in Jesus.

Son (vv. 46, 48).

There are two sons in this lection. The one is the "son of Timaeus." This is the poor, blind begger living in poverty and misery. He represents the human lot. The other son is the "Son of David." He is the divine person, who as David's son, is the promised Messiah who has come in Jesus. Here we have a son of man, and

Son of God. The "Son of David" is a messianic title, for the messiah was to be the son of David. It is the first and only time in Mark that this title is used for Jesus. Also, it is the first time that the term was not rebuked nor denied by Jesus. The messianic secret was out! When the Messiah comes, the eyes of the blind would be opened. (Isaiah 35:5) Jesus' healing the blind man was evidence of his being "Son of David."

Silent (v. 48).

The crowd scolded and rebuked Bartimaeus for his yelling. We can hear them say with anger, "For God's sake, shut up!" Why did they want silence? It may have been because the noise of his loud crying prevented them from hearing what Jesus was saying as they walked to Jerusalem. The people did not want to miss a word that he said. On the other hand, maybe it was fear that demanded silence. He was yelling, "Son of David." It was a nationalist slogan which could result in a riot and bring Roman troops.

Mantle (v. 50).

When Bartimaeus received the call to go to Jesus, he threw down his mantle or cloak. It indicated that he wanted to be free from anything that might retard his speed in reaching Jesus for healing. The dropping of the mantle symbolized his eagerness to get light into his life. Moreover, the dropping of the mantle may have meant that he was dropping his old life of darkness, misery and poverty for a new life of sight, employment and security.

Call (v. 49).

Jesus said to those around him, "Call him." Why didn't Jesus go to him? How could, except with difficulty and human assistance, a blind man come to him? Is Jesus teaching a lesson here? No one comes to Jesus on his own steam or by his own decision. A person is called to come to Jesus. In this case, Jesus himself gave the call. But, note that the call came through people. Today his call can come in and through the people of the church. Now, when Jesus is at the right hand of God, people are called to come to Jesus by the Holy Spirit.

Well (v. 52).

The Greek word used here is *sozein*, meaning both healing and salvation. In one sense, there was physical healing because

Bartimaeus was cured of his blindness. Also, there was salvation that came to him. As a result of the miracle, Bartimaeus became a disciple who followed Jesus to Jerusalem. Perhaps he was one who witnessed the trial before Pilate, the nailing to the Cross, and the glorious Resurrection. He could see all this because now his eyes could see.

Application

Relevance of Revelation.
   1. Two Kinds of Blindness. Today's miracle deals with physical blindness, which Jesus was able to cure. We do not expect this type of healing in our time. However, there are miracles of curing blindness that can and do happen through medical science and exceptional experiences. There is another type of blindness that is more serious. It is spiritual blindness, the lack of vision, the failure of insight and the insensitivitiy to values. Though blind, Bartimaeus had spiritual vision in his ability to see Jesus as the source of his cure. This miracle, therefore, is relevant to both kinds of blindness existing in our day.
   2. Spiritual Vision. The miracle of healing a blind man has relevance to our lives because the case and example of Bartimaeus can teach us much about our own spiritual sight. His faith in the mercy and power of Jesus inspires us to have similar faith in finding Christ as the solution to our problems. There is also his persistence. No one could stop him, nor stop his repeated pleas for mercy. Since we are prone to give up praying, there is a lesson here for us. Bartimaeus was one who knew what he wanted and needed. Do we need what we want? The story comes to a climax when, out of gratitude, he becomes a follower of Jesus. Not all who Jesus healed became disciples. The miracle's relevance for us today centers upon our need for vision, for faith in Jesus as Messiah, for persistence in prayer and for discipleship.

Sermon Suggestions.
   1. Sight Become Light. Are we spiritually blind because we are in the darkness of unbelief and sin? We can have the best of physical eyes, but we must have light to see. Christ called himself the light of the world. To be able to see truth, to see our own sinfulness, to see the saviorhood in the Savior, we need Christ to illustrate our minds and lives.

2. "O Say, Can You See?" Often a prophet when called by God was asked, "What do you see?" Can you see yourself as a sinner needing mercy? Can you see the saviorhood in Jesus? Can you see yourself as a disciple of Jesus? Can you see the needs of the world? If not, you are in need of a miracle to open your eyes.

3. Mercy, Mercy! When Bartimaeus cried out, he did not beg for sight, nor for money. He repeatedly cried out for mercy, "Jesus, have mercy on me." Because he did not specify his needs, Jesus asked, "What do you want me to do for you?" It is mercy and not justice that we need. In worship we use the Kyrie — "Lord, have mercy . . . Christ, have mercy." Like Bartimaeus, we say or sing it repeatedly to express persistence and earnestness. We sing, "There's a wideness in God's mercy." In a congregational prayer, we say, "Lord, in your mercy, hear our prayer." It is only when we are in need, when we realize our hopelessness and helplessness that we cry out for mercy.

4. The Walls of Blindness. Blindness is like walls that shut the blind off from the world. They must live in darkness. Because of their inability to make a living, they must beg for food. How humiliating! It means extreme poverty and social isolation behind the walls of blindness. For Bartimaeus the walls of blindness fell, just as the walls of Jericho fell at the time of Joshua. The walls of Jericho fell down when the Israelites walked around the walls each day for six days. On the seventh day, they marched around the walls seven times with horns blowing and people shouting. Bartimaeus used a similar strategy. He persisted in calling for help. He shouted for mercy. The walls of blindness fell when Jesus called him to come. The walls fell by the power of God responding to the persistent cries of his people.

5. Your Faith. Bartimaeus is a study in faith. Jesus said to him, "Your faith has made you well." It was his faith that resulted in his getting his sight. He had faith that Jesus was the Messiah who was to bring sight to the blind. His faith was expressed in his persistent cries for mercy. His faith was expressed in following Jesus to Jerusalem.

6. An Indirect Call of Christ. The call of God does not always come directly from God. It may come indirectly through people. In the case of Bartimaeus, the call to come to Jesus came through people. Jesus did not go to the blind man. Nor did he call him to come to him. Rather, he sent disciples to go to Bartimaeus and tell him to come. The call of Christ may come through other people. This may be a church official's invitation to serve as a teacher or committee member. The call may be a congregational election to a position of leadership. A pastor may receive a call of God to serve a congregation through a congregation's election.

7. *Now or Never.* Bartimaeus teaches us to follow his example in seizing an opportunity when it comes. He heard Jesus and his company passing by on his final journey to Jerusalem. Never again would Jesus come to Jericho. It was now or never to get Jesus' healing. Now was his chance to receive sight. As soon as he learned that Jesus was passing by, he began his noisy appeal. He would not miss this opportunity lest he have to live the rest of his life in darkness.

8. *Want or Need?* What we want we may not need. What we need we may not want. When Bartimaeus came to Jesus, he was asked, "What do you want me to do for you?" Bartimaeus said he wanted what he needed, eyesight. This can be a crucial question for each person: "What do you want Jesus to do for you?" Are you sure that what you want is what you need? Is your need for faith, for more love, for forgiveness?

9. *Never too Busy.* Bartimaeus is one more illustration that Jesus is never too busy to help one in need. He was headed for Jerusalem. He had only fifteen more miles to walk. He wanted to get there for the Passover and to make his formal entry into the city as the nation's prospective king. Although his Disciples tried to quiet Bartimaeus so that Jesus would not be delayed, Jesus heard the cries and stopped to see what he could do for him. No matter how busy Christ is running the universe while seated at the right hand of his Father, no matter how many millions cry for help, he is ready to hear and respond to the cry of the needy.

Sermon Structures.

1. When Christ Calls! (vv. 46-52). What happens when Christ calls a person? What does one do? How does one react? Bartimaeus serves as an example.

A. Shut up! — "telling him to be silent" — v. 48

B. Stand up! — "he sprang up" — v. 50

C. Speak up! — "What do you want me to do for you?" — v. 51

2. A Faith That Wins (vv. 46-52). Bartimaeus had a faith that gained his sight. Jesus said, "Your faith has made you well." What was the nature of his faith? What kind of faith wins the favor of Christ?

A. Faith in the power of Christ to help — v. 47

B. Faith expressed in persistence — v. 48

C. Faith shown in discipleship — v. 52

3. On Becoming a Disciple (vv. 46-52). How does one become a disciple of Jesus? Is it in joining a church? Is it in holding Jesus in highest respect? Bartimaeus shows us how to:

A. Seize the opportunity — v. 47

B. See the Messiah in Jesus ("Son of David") — v. 47

C. Respond to his call — v. 50

D. Follow Jesus even to death — v. 52

4. The Traveling Healer (vv. 46-52). Jesus was traveling to Jerusalem and was passing through Jericho. He was on his way to offer himself as Savior to the nation. Although his face was like a flint in his determination to get to the holy city, where he knew he would suffer and die, he had time to stop and respond to a blind beggar's cry for mercy. What we learn about Jesus:

A. Jesus is never too busy to help — v. 49

B. Jesus is concerned about the least — v. 46

C. Jesus is able to do the impossible — vv. 51, 52

5. Do You Need What You Want? (v. 51). Jesus asked Bartimaeus, "What do you want me to do for you?" He wanted what he needed. Often we want what we do not need.

A. Do you need what you want?

B. Do you want what you need?

6. What Would a Beggar Want? (v. 51). As Luther said in his dying hour, all of us are beggars. We come to Jesus as beggars and Jesus asks what he can do for us. To answer this calls for self-understanding. It shows what our priorities are. Why would Jesus ask this of a beggar? What would you expect a blind person to want or need other than his sight? What do you want Jesus to do for you?

A. Do you want more faith?

B. Do you want to know the truth of God?

C. Do you want vision and insight?

D. Do you want more love for Christ?

Illustration

A Modern Miracle.

A man, aged sixty-two, had been blind for nine years. He was in his back yard when a thunderstorm began. "I heard a sound like a whip cracking over my head," he recalls. "Next thing I knew I woke up facedown in the mud." He went to his bedroom where his wife found him later. He told her he had been hit by lightning and asked for a drink. Then he began shouting, "I can see you! I can see the house! I can see!" His doctor said, "I don't know why he can see again. All that I know is that he was blind. And now he isn't."

Blindness a Blessing?

Fanny Crosby who wrote 6,000 gospel songs, was blinded by an illness at the age of six weeks. When a friend expressed sympathy for her condition, she quickly replied, "Do you know that if at birth I had been able to make one petition, it would have been that I should be born blind?" "Why?" asked the surprised friend. "Because when I get to heaven, the first face that shall ever gladden my sight will be that of my Savior!"

What Do You Want?

Some years ago a newspaper correspondent spent New Year's Eve with American troops in South Korea. The temperature that night was forty-two degrees below zero. Eighteen hundred Marines were facing 100,000 Communist troops. At midnight, supper was served to the men; it consisted of cold beans, which had to be eaten out of cans while standing beside the tanks. The correspondent noticed a huge Marine whose clothes had frozen as hard as a board. His beard was encrusted with mud, and his hands were blue from the cold. He was eating his ice-cold beans with a trench knife. The newsman asked him, "If I were God and could give you one thing you'd rather have than anything in the world, what would you ask for?" The Marine thought about it for a while and finally said, "I would ask you to give me tomorrow."

Missed Opportunity.

Bartimaeus seized the opportunity to get help from Jesus. Many years ago the Coca-Cola company had an opportunity to buy twice-bankrupt Pepsi-Cola. The owner was willing to sell for $1,000. But, since Coke at the time had a monopoly on the soft drink business, Coke rejected the offer to buy the company — which is now its main competitor.

Persistence.

One of the secrets of Bartimaeus' success was his persistence. His call for mercy could not be stopped. Years ago a man bought a gold mine for $300,000. After digging for several years, he did not get enough gold to meet his expenses. He sold the mine. After only six hours of drilling, the new company discovered one of the purest pockets of gold ever found in North America. The former owner had been only six inches away from the find.

Vision.

J. D. Adams said, "Ours is a generation surfeited with facts and starved for vision."

John Masefield said that the difference between his life at sea and in the carpet mill at Yonkers was that in the mill he "missed the companionship of the sky."

About 350 years ago a shipload of travelers landed on the northeast coast of America. The first year they established a town site. The next year they instituted the town government. The third year the town government planned to build a road five miles westward into the wilderness. In the fourth year the people tried to impeach their town government because they thought it was a waste of public funds to build a road five miles westward into a wilderness. Who needed to go there anyway? At one time they had had the vision to cross 3,000 miles of ocean and endure great hardships to reach their destination. Within a few years they had lost the vision to go five miles into the wilderness.

A Call Through People.

Jesus called Bartimaeus to himself through the people around him. There was once a mid-west pastor who was recruiting a person to be superintendent of the Sunday school. The pastor was immediately turned down. Then the pastor asked, "Would you do it for the church?" "No." "Would you do it for the good of the community?" "No." "Would you do it for me, your pastor?" "No." Finally, the pastor desperately asked, "Well, would you do it for Jesus?" The lady thought a moment and then exploded, "Damn it! You know I would have to do it for Jesus!"